Partnerships in Educati
Collaborations for Student Success

"50 USEFUL THINGS TO KNOW ABOUT SCHOOL PARTNERSHIPS"

Graeme Lawrie MBE

Partnerships between schools and community organisations can be powerful tools for improving student outcomes.

In this reference book, we explore the various forms that partnerships can take, including business partnerships, community partnerships, and parent partnerships.

We also delve into the benefits and challenges of establishing and maintaining these collaborations.

Table of Contents

1: Introduction to partnerships in education
2: Business partnerships
3: Community partnerships
4: Parent partnerships
5: Challenges and solutions
6: Impact reporting
7: Using social media to support partnerships
8: Engaging school staff in partnerships work
9: Staffing a partnerships department in school
10: Engaging senior management and trustees
11: Budgeting for partnerships
12: The importance of data analysis in partnerships
13: Change management in partnerships
14: Resource management in partnerships
15: Building relationships with local schools
16: Impact reporting in partnerships
17: Partnerships in schools and service learning
18: Local, national and international partnerships
19: Maintaining relationships in partnerships
20: Budgets in partnerships
21: Sustaining partnerships
22: Communicating with different stakeholders
23: Planning a framework for partnerships
24: Community members who oppose partnerships
25: Explaining schools in partnerships
26: Charitable status and the use of charitable funding
27: Safeguarding in partnerships
28: Risk assessments in partnerships
29: Useful resources for partnerships
30: Outreach or partnerships
31: Marketing in partnerships
32: Succession planning in partnerships
33: Approaching local businesses for support

34: Investing in children from other schools
35: Replacing core services
36: Top 10 questions asked by partnerships staff
37: Fundraising for partnerships in education
38: Matching partnerships activity to the curriculum
39: Targeting real disadvantage and underprivilege
40: Partnerships and diversity
41: The best characteristics and skills of staff
42: Avoiding the 'Robin Hood' approach to partnerships
43: Bringing the school board on the journey
44: Convincing finance to support partnerships
45: How can school staff get involved in partnerships?
46: Involving teachers/support staff and students
47: What is an MOU
48: What is a Partnerships Agreement?
49: Resilience in partnerships staffing
50: Transport issues in partnerships

Conclusion

Welcome: A resource for my colleagues

This book is the culmination of countless discussions and exchanges with colleagues spanning the past decade. Reflecting on the inquiries I've encountered, many of the answers remain consistent over time.

However, I can't help but wonder how many individuals in new partnership roles lack the opportunity to connect with seasoned professionals.

I've curated this reference book, aiming to provide guidance to those embarking on their own partnership journey. Organised into 50 topics commonly discussed, each section offers a concise and accessible snapshot of an answer.

Designed to be light and easily navigable, this book prioritises simplicity without sacrificing substance. My hope is that readers can find answers swiftly, empowering them to navigate the complexities of partnerships with confidence.

Should anyone wish to delve deeper or engage in further discussion, I extend an open invitation. Whether through a virtual Zoom call or a face-to-face coffee chat, I'm here to offer support and insights.

In the meantime, I trust this book serves as a valuable companion on your partnerships journey. Best wishes for your endeavours ahead.

Graeme Lawrie MBE

1: Introduction

Partnerships between schools and community organisations can be a powerful tool for improving student outcomes. These collaborations can take many forms, including business partnerships, community partnerships, and parent partnerships.

In this section, we will provide an overview of the different types of partnerships that schools can form and the ways in which these collaborations can support student learning and development.

Business partnerships: involve schools working with local businesses to provide resources, mentorship, and real-world learning opportunities for students. These partnerships can be beneficial for both the school and the business, as they provide a way for businesses to give back to the community and for schools to access resources and expertise that they may not have otherwise.

Community partnerships: involve schools working with community organisations to address issues such as poverty, inequality, and social isolation. These partnerships can be beneficial for both the school and the community, as they provide a way for the school to address the needs of its students and for the community to have a positive impact on the education system.

Parent partnerships: involve engaging parents in the educational process and building strong relationships between the school and the home. These partnerships can be beneficial for both the school and the parents, as they provide a way for parents to support their

children's learning and for the school to tap into the expertise and resources of the parent community.
In the following sections, we will delve more deeply into each of these types of partnerships and explore the benefits and challenges of establishing and maintaining these collaborations.

What are partnerships?

Partnerships are collaborations between schools and community organisations that aim to support student learning and development, address community needs, and foster positive relationships between schools and the wider community. Partnerships can take many forms, such as service-learning initiatives, community schools, business partnerships, and cultural exchange programs.

Partnerships can be beneficial for both schools and community organisations, as they provide opportunities for shared learning and resources, and can help to address complex social and community issues in a more comprehensive and sustainable way. Partnerships can also support student learning and development by providing real-world experiences and connections to the community.

However, partnerships require careful planning and management to be successful. It is important for schools and community organisations to clearly define the goals and objectives of the partnership, to establish clear roles and responsibilities for all stakeholders, and to have systems in place for monitoring and evaluating the impact of the partnership.

This book aims to provide simple and straight forward guidance and insights for educators and community leaders looking to build and maintain strong partnerships between schools and community organisations. Through a combination of research and practical examples, the book covers a range of topics, including how to identify potential partners, how to engage stakeholders, how to manage resources, how to measure impact, and how to sustain partnerships over time.

There are various models of school partnerships that can be used to create strong collaborations and promote student success. Some of the most common models include:

Twinning: This model involves a partnership between two schools, typically in different countries, where students and staff can exchange ideas, cultures, and best practices. This type of partnership can be beneficial for both students and staff as it allows them to gain a broader understanding of different cultures and perspectives.

Curriculum-based partnerships: This model involves a partnership between schools that focuses on the development and implementation of specific curriculum or educational programs. This type of partnership can be beneficial for students as it allows them to gain access to a wider range of educational opportunities and resources.

Service-learning partnerships: This model involves a partnership between schools and community organisations where students are provided with opportunities to engage in service-learning projects.

These projects can be used to address community needs while also providing students with hands-on learning experiences.

Professional development partnerships: This model involves a partnership between schools and educational institutions or organisations where teachers and staff can access professional development opportunities. This can help to ensure that teachers and staff are equipped with the latest knowledge and skills to support student success.

Mentoring partnerships: This model involves a partnership between schools where older students are matched with younger students as mentors. This type of partnership can be beneficial for both students as it allows the older students to develop leadership skills and the younger students to gain support and guidance.

Virtual partnerships: This model involves a partnership between schools that utilises technology, such as video conferencing, to connect students and staff from different locations. This type of partnership can be beneficial for students as it allows them to gain access to a wider range of educational resources and opportunities.

There are various models of school partnerships that can be used to create strong collaborations and promote student success. Each model has its own unique benefits and can be tailored to meet the specific needs and goals of the partnership.

Implementation in real-world scenarios
Every partnership program is inherently unique. Different schools, with varying values, facilities, staffing structures, timetables, and financial resources, approach partnership initiatives in distinct ways.

Some partnership programs are highly successful with only two schools involved, while others encompass collaborations among multiple institutions. There are even a few programs operating at a grand scale, involving hundreds of schools.

None of these approaches are inherently incorrect; each holds its own value. The crux of the matter lies in the necessity to avoid making assumptions and, instead, craft a comprehensive strategy for partnership programs based on diligent research.

The crucial initial year of any new partnership endeavour should be dedicated to thorough groundwork, which includes studying Ofsted reports, visiting schools, engaging in conversations with senior leaders, and analysing publicly available data, such as the Income Deprivation Affecting Children Index (IDACI).

Collaborating with the local authorities is imperative, as it provides insights into areas where the program could make a significant impact. Additionally, delving into data related to employment, salaries, educational attainment, free school meals, pupil premium, and other pertinent information is vital.

If a successful partnership group exists nearby, exploring the possibility of joining forces aligns with our belief in 'collaboration over competition,' with the best interests of the children at the forefront. A frequently asked question pertains to financial allocation and staffing resources: 'How much financial investment should we dedicate to this?' or 'How many staff hours should be allocated?'

Answers to these questions should ascend to the board level for deliberation, taking into account the organisation's capacity and ambition to engage in this endeavour. Naturally, considerations regarding charitable status, not-for-profit classification, and balancing operational costs with capital projects will arise.

The pivotal focus should be on developing a well-defined strategy that outlines the course of action. Contemplate a five-year model and establish clear outcomes. An effective approach to this process is employing a 'Theory of Change (ToC)'

"Methodology: 'The Theory of Change (ToC) is a methodological framework used across various sectors, including business, philanthropy, not-for-profit organisations, international development, research, and government, to facilitate social change. It begins by defining the long-term goals of a social program and then works backward to identify the necessary preconditions for success."

Consider short-term, medium-term, and long-term outcomes for your program while constructing an outcome pathway. Assess your organisation's existing strengths, weaknesses, potential opportunities, and threats to success through a SWOT analysis.

These established outcomes will serve as the foundation for future impact reporting, providing key performance indicators (KPIs) for your partnership initiatives.

The amalgamation of each initiative will contribute to this overarching strategy, facilitating seamless reporting to various stakeholders, and allowing for course adjustments through regular monitoring and evaluation.

2: Business partnerships

Business partnerships involve schools working with local businesses to provide resources, mentorship, and real-world learning opportunities for students.

These partnerships can be beneficial for both the school and the business, as they provide a way for businesses to give back to the community and for schools to access resources and expertise that they may not have otherwise. There are many ways that businesses can partner with schools. Some examples include:

- Donating resources, such as books, computers, or other materials
- Providing mentorship or internships for students
- Offering job shadowing or career exploration opportunities
- Hosting events or workshops on topics related to the business
- Participating in school events or volunteering as a guest speaker

Business partnerships can be a win-win for both parties. Schools benefit from the resources and expertise that businesses bring to the table, while businesses can benefit from the opportunity to connect with future employees and customers.

However, it is important for schools and businesses to communicate clearly and establish clear goals and expectations for the partnership to ensure that it is successful.

In the next section, we will explore community partnerships and the ways in which schools can work with community organisations to address important issues and support student learning and development.

Implementation in real-world scenarios
Industry engagement holds a pivotal role in educational partnerships, displaying a resounding enthusiasm to collaborate with the educational sector to enrich and secure future talent.

These industries often possess dedicated 'Corporate Social Responsibility' (CSR) or 'Environmental, Social, and Governance' (ESG) funds, which can be channelled towards supporting educational programs. Smaller companies may contribute donations or establish modest initiatives to assist schools, while larger organisations may allocate entire teams with educational specialists committed to this endeavour.

For educational institutions, gaining access to these funds can present a challenge, as educators may not be entirely familiar with corporate environments. The distinct language utilised, the necessity to construct robust business cases and proposals, and the creation of comprehensive presentations or 'decks' for senior management or board members can be a daunting prospect.

Irrespective of the approach taken, one paramount objective remains: the cultivation of trust in both you and your plans. Donors must have confidence that their financial contributions will not only be effectively utilised but will also yield maximum educational value.

Furthermore, the manner in which this impact is reported should enable donors to convey the results to their senior management and board members while facilitating financial reporting. Consequently, it becomes evident that the larger the financial support sought, the greater the need for substantiated evidence and a well-established proof of concept to instil faith in the budget-holders.

The most effective route to achieving this is by implementing a well-structured program, grounded in the research and data outlined in the previous section, with easily measurable and profound outcomes. The successful execution of events, coupled with the adept utilisation of the resulting outputs as collateral assets for future sponsorships, becomes imperative.

This includes the collection of testimonials, high-quality photographs and videos, survey data, press coverage, and more. Ensuring that prior donors are prominently featured in all social media and press releases serves as a compelling showcase for prospective donors, illustrating the benefits they can expect from collaborating with your institution.

Over time, a repository of 'proof of concept' and 'digital assets' will be amassed. This not only equips you with the ability to narrate a compelling story about your proposed endeavours but also substantiates it with tangible evidence of past successes.

You can cite examples of how previous partnerships have benefitted companies, thus enhancing the appeal of your proposal. It is crucial to recognise that sponsorship or support need not be solely financial.

Having a well-known, prominent organisation affiliated with your event, even in name, can attract support from others in various forms, such as resources, facilities, advice, and mentorship.

3: Community partnerships

Community partnerships involve schools working with community organisations to address issues such as poverty, inequality, and social isolation.

These partnerships can be beneficial for both the school and the community, as they provide a way for the school to address the needs of its students and for the community to have a positive impact on the education system.

There are many ways that schools can partner with community organisations. Some examples include:

- Partnering with non-profits or community groups to provide services such as tutoring, mentorship, or extracurricular activities.
- Working with local businesses to provide resources or funding for school programs.

- Collaborating with community leaders to advocate for education issues and policies.
- Participating in community service projects or volunteering as a group

Community partnerships can be an effective way for schools to meet the needs of their students and address issues that may be affecting their learning.

However, it is important for schools and community organisations to communicate clearly and establish clear goals and expectations for the partnership to ensure that it is successful.

In the next section, we will explore parent partnerships and the ways in which schools can engage parents in the educational process to support student learning and success.

Implementation in real-world scenarios

As is the case with all partnership activities, community partnerships will exhibit uniqueness in every location, contingent upon your specific locality.

Typically, there exist networks encompassing diverse entities such as young carers, refugee support initiatives, charity shops (such as Oxfam and Cancer Research), Cubs, Scouts, Guides, local church groups, and various other community organisations.

Additionally, numerous regional charities are always open to supporting fundraising efforts and volunteering initiatives. Once again, the key lies in diligent research and investing time in building networks. Commencing with the local authority can be a solid starting point for gaining insights into community groups.

However, one should not underestimate the significance of the modest town notice board and the unassuming piece of paper inviting you to local meetings or events. A substantial portion of a partnership leader's role involves not only researching these communities but actively participating in their meetings and gaining an in-depth understanding of their goals.

Only through this process can you align your own objectives and identify potential intersections that can enrich educational endeavours across the region. By forging connections with these communities, you not only acquire a valuable resource for future collaborations but also establish a prominent presence within the broader community beyond the educational institution.

People will begin to refer individuals with innovative ideas to you, and you will receive invitations to gatherings, negating the need for constant seeking. This, in turn, cultivates and nurtures a positive image of your institution within the community. We continually emphasise the importance of building trust and demonstrating a proof of concept.

Soon, word will spread that your intentions are genuine, devoid of ulterior motives, and that you are a force for the betterment of all. Moreover, it is essential, although not necessarily an immediate consideration, to ensure that you have the capacity to deliver on your promises. Underpromising and overdelivering, where feasible, should be a guiding principle. Trust can be as fragile as it is valuable, and consistently positive interactions leading to shared outcomes are paramount.

4: Parent partnerships

Parent partnerships involve engaging parents in the educational process and building strong relationships between the school and the home.

These partnerships can be beneficial for both the school and the parents, as they provide a way for parents to support their children's learning and for the school to tap into the expertise and resources of the parent community.

There are many ways that schools can partner with parents. Some examples include:

- Involving parents in decision-making and policy development
- Providing opportunities for parents to volunteer at the school or participate in school events.
- Offering parent education programs or workshops on topics such as child development or effective parenting strategies
- Facilitating communication between the school and the home through newsletters, parent-teacher conferences, or other forms of outreach

Parent partnerships can be an effective way for schools to involve parents in the educational process and build stronger relationships with the families of their students. However, it is important for schools to be sensitive to the diverse needs and schedules of parents and to provide multiple ways for them to be involved in their children's learning.

In the next section, we will address some of the common challenges that schools may face when establishing and maintaining partnerships, and we will provide strategies for overcoming these challenges and maximising the benefits of these collaborations.

Implementation in real-world scenarios
Parents wield considerable influence and offer valuable resources in various capacities. Many parents are enthusiastically eager to engage in their children's school activities and educational journey. Furthermore, a substantial number of parents appreciate the opportunity to connect with their peers and become a part of a community, thereby contributing positively to their overall well-being.

Numerous parents are in professions that they can discuss at career fairs; some might hold roles within these professions that grant them access to valuable resources and facilities, which they are willing to share.

Additionally, parents may bring unique expertise and experiences to the table, making them valuable candidates for guest speaker roles or providing support for ongoing educational initiatives.

Several schools incorporate a checkbox in their parental sign-up forms at the start of each school year, granting permission for contact regarding these opportunities. Consequently, a partnerships lead has the responsibility not only to initiate contact, engage in conversations, and extend invitations for coffee but also to establish a distinctive rapport with these parents.

Maintaining these connections and keeping parents informed about your institution's capacity are equally crucial aspects of the role. The frequency of reaching out to parents holds paramount significance. Striking the right balance is essential, as you do not want to inundate them with constant requests, yet you also want to ensure they do not feel neglected due to infrequent contact.

The introduction of a partnerships parent committee offers a solution to manage these connections efficiently. Conducting one or two meetings per term, where the partnerships lead provides updates on future plans, and a parental chair solicits support, facilitates a collaborative approach.

These meetings are open to all parents, and the addition of tea or a glass of wine often enhances the atmosphere. Empowering parents to take ownership of partnership activities not only eases the burden of communication but also cultivates advocates for your partnership initiatives. Involving parents in the process and making them integral to the journey is essential.

A robust partnerships parent group can provide substantial resources, provided you invest the necessary time to foster this community. It is imperative to ensure that their role remains supportive rather than strategic leadership. Consistent and transparent meetings with the partnerships lead can help ensure that their contributions align with the intended goals of the partnership program.

5: Challenges and solutions

While partnerships between schools and community organisations can be a powerful tool for improving student outcomes, it is important to recognise that establishing and maintaining these collaborations can be challenging.

Some common challenges that schools may face include:

Lack of time or resources: Both schools and community organisations may be stretched thin, making it difficult to find the time and resources to invest in partnerships.

Misaligned goals or expectations: It is important for schools and community organisations to establish clear goals and expectations for the partnership. If these are misaligned, it can lead to misunderstandings and frustration.

Communication breakdown: Effective communication is key to the success of any partnership. If there are breakdowns in communication, it can lead to misunderstandings and hinder the effectiveness of the collaboration.

Differences in culture or perspective: Schools and community organisations may come from different backgrounds and have different perspectives, which can lead to misunderstandings or conflicts. To overcome these challenges and maximise the benefits of partnerships, schools can take the following steps:

Establish clear goals and expectations: Both parties should be clear about what they hope to achieve through the partnership and how they will work together to achieve those goals.

Communicate effectively: It is important to establish regular channels of communication and to make an effort to understand each other's perspectives and needs.

Foster a sense of collaboration: Schools and community organisations should work together as partners, rather than as separate entities. This requires a shared sense of ownership and a willingness to collaborate and find solutions together.

Seek out resources and support: Schools can seek out resources and support from external organisations to help with the challenges of establishing and maintaining partnerships. By addressing these challenges and building strong partnerships, schools can create positive and lasting impacts on the learning and development of their students.

Implementation in real-world scenarios

It is a commonplace scenario for a teacher to find themselves thrust into a new role as a Partnerships Lead, armed with nothing but their teaching background. Suddenly, they must adapt swiftly to a markedly different way of working. Teachers in the state sector are often unfamiliar with the practices in the independent sector, and vice versa.

Therefore, the establishment of equitable and robust connections between organisations becomes paramount before any concrete plans can be developed. Furthermore, it is a frequent challenge that the budget and allocated time for partnership activities can be quite restrictive.

Given the multifaceted nature of networking, strategic planning, research, and relationship building, the role of a Partnerships lead can be all-encompassing. Undertaking a comprehensive approach within a few hours each week is typically impractical. Consequently, organisations must carefully assess their ambitions in this regard.

Additionally, it is common for Partnerships leads to downplay the costs associated with activities in an effort to ensure their feasibility. The often-used phrase, 'it's only a few teas and coffees,' is a mere fraction of the expenses to consider. Staff time, consumables, catering, security, parking, and various other factors should be taken into account.

Even a simple meeting with colleagues from different schools can generate a day's worth of administrative work through calls and emails. Hence, it is imperative to adopt a realistic approach from the outset. Present the actual costs of events and link them to impact reporting for effective analysis of potential outcomes in relation to overall expenses.

This evaluation will facilitate informed decisions about whether the proposed activity is worthwhile or if funds should be reallocated to more impactful endeavours. Partnerships leads should allocate time to collaborate with their counterparts in other schools, charities, universities, or companies.

They must ensure clarity of goals and expectations within the group and establish aligned leadership. It's worth noting that colleagues in the state sector may not have the same time or resources as those in the independent sector, making equitable relationship management challenging but not insurmountable.

The success of a partnerships network consistently hinges on effective communication. Ensuring that all leaders within the partnership have the opportunity to become well-acquainted and discuss ongoing plans, as well as future prospects, is essential. Constructing the strategy collectively, with each stakeholder taking ownership, is beneficial.

Defining organisation-specific goals and expectations, alongside shared objectives, constitutes the foundation of a successful plan.

Documenting these goals and expectations not only aids in assessing activities against outcomes but also serves as a valuable component of an annual evaluation, gauging the partnership group's success. Incorporating a third party into these meetings ensures transparency and openness, providing an equal voice to all stakeholders.

6: Impact reporting
In this section, we will explore the importance of impact reporting in partnerships between schools and community organisations. Impact reporting is the process of collecting and analysing data to understand the impact of a particular initiative or program.

By collecting and analysing data, schools and community organisations can better understand the effectiveness of their partnerships and identify areas for improvement.

Impact reporting is an important part of any partnership because it allows schools and community organisations to understand whether their efforts are having the desired impact on students. It can also help to build trust between partners and demonstrate the value of the partnership to external stakeholders, such as funders and policy makers.

There are many different ways to collect and analyse data for impact reporting, including:

Surveys: Surveys can be used to gather feedback from students, teachers, and other stakeholders about the partnership and its impact.

Focus groups: Focus groups can be used to gather more in-depth information about the partnership and its impact from a smaller group of participants.

Observations: Observations can be used to gather data about the partnership in action and how it is impacting students.

Data analysis: Schools and community organisations can also analyse existing data, such as test scores or attendance records, to understand the impact of the partnership.

Impact reporting is an ongoing process and should be a regular part of any partnership. By collecting and analysing data on a regular basis, schools and community organisations can continually improve their partnerships and better support student learning and development.

Implementation in real-world scenarios
Impact reporting practices can vary significantly across different organisations. The approach to impact reporting is influenced by several factors, including the nature of the partnership group, the scale of the work, the schools involved, and their respective values.

However, one element that should remain consistent is your strategy document and the outcome statements. After completing a 'Theory of Change' and establishing the desired end goals, you can work backward through your strategy, utilising this data to prepare for data collection, assessment, and evaluation of your work.

Some schools choose to manage this process through Excel documents, while others opt for online survey tools. Some may invest in third-party impact assessment tools, while some develop their own systems.

Regardless of the system employed, what truly matters is the commitment to assessing impact and conducting regular evaluations. It is equally crucial to maintain consistency in the assessment process. You should be able to assess multiple initiatives in the same manner, ensuring that the data collected is reliable for comparing activities.

When collecting data, consider various fields, including the overall cost (comprising resources and staff), the educational enhancements brought about by the initiative, the subject disciplines addressed, and areas of the national curriculum covered.

You might even wish to connect the outcomes and assessment data to census or inspection criteria.

Regardless of the specific data fields you select, you should be able to answer a fundamental question: How did you achieve your outcomes, or conversely, what needs improvement? Based on this data, you can assess how to adapt future events to enhance their effectiveness.

For example, you may realise that you have focused too much on local initiatives rather than international ones. You might discover that you've engaged more with foundation-year students and less with upper school students.

In such cases, you can naturally adjust your efforts to align with the specific outcomes you initially set. The output from your impact reporting should be valuable for communicating with various stakeholders, including teachers within your schools, parents, the board of directors, or even the general public via social media and the school website.

Celebrating success and incorporating these achievements into your communication strategy is essential. It not only builds trust but also serves as a consistent reminder of the meaningful work you are undertaking and its purpose.

7: Using social media to support partnerships
In this section, we will explore the role that social media can play in supporting partnerships between schools and community organisations. With the proliferation of social media platforms, it is easier than

ever for schools and community organisations to connect and collaborate online.

There are many ways that schools and community organisations can use social media to support their partnerships:

Communicate with partners: Social media can be an effective way to stay in touch with partners and share updates, news, and resources.

Promote the partnership: Schools and community organisations can use social media to promote their partnership and share information about the initiatives and programs they are working on.

Engage with stakeholders: Social media can be a powerful tool for engaging with stakeholders, such as students, parents, and community members. Schools and community organisations can use social media to gather feedback, ideas, and support for their partnerships.

Connect with other organisations: Social media can also be a way for schools and community organisations to connect with other organisations and find new partners.

When using social media to support partnerships, it is important for schools and community organisations to be transparent, responsive, and respectful. It is also important to be mindful of privacy and security concerns.

By using social media in a strategic and responsible way, schools and community organisations can strengthen their partnerships and better serve their students and communities.

Implementation in real-world scenarios
The utilisation of social media in partnership work holds immense potential. It not only disseminates your initiatives to the wider world but also establishes your organisation as dedicated to skills and knowledge acquisition, charitable endeavours, social mobility, and public benefit.

This, in conjunction with evidence of successful initiatives, fosters trust among organisations and underscores your commitment to actively promoting partnerships with them.

Various social media platforms are available, including X, LinkedIn, Instagram, Snapchat, and more. Each platform serves a distinct purpose, and crafting a strategy for conveying your narrative on each is essential. X, Instagram, and Snapchat are particularly effective for sharing immediate brief updates with followers about developments in your partnership initiatives.

LinkedIn takes it a step further by facilitating interactions, enabling you to connect with others, engage in meaningful conversations, and share thought pieces beneficial to your audience.

The pivotal question lies in how many resources, both time and financial, you allocate to social media on a daily basis. You can opt for professional accounts on platforms like LinkedIn and invest in added functionality on X. Promoting posts through financial backing and employing analytics can provide valuable insights into your audience, including when they are typically online, the types of posts they find valuable (such as photos being essential on X), their geographic location, device usage, and more.

However, social media goes beyond merely sharing events; it is a networking tool that opens doors to valuable networking opportunities. Following influential figures in your field and actively engaging with their posts not only brings you to their attention but also to their followers.

The strategic use of tagging individuals and incorporating relevant hashtags is another means of increasing your exposure. By thoughtfully monitoring trending themes, you can ride the wave of interest with minimal extra effort.

Automation plays a significant role in managing social media effectively. Applications like Zapier or IFTTT allow you to cross-post on multiple platforms simultaneously. Additionally, you can set up notifications to stay informed when others mention you in their posts.

Being prompt and responsive on social media is a valuable skill to cultivate. Effectively managing notifications, sharing interesting and meaningful content, and knowing when and how to engage with others' posts can distinguish you as a leader in the digital landscape.

Dedicating daily time to social media is a worthwhile investment, and ensuring regular communication with your marketing department to align with their posts and social media contributions can enhance the impact of your messaging.

8: Engaging school staff in partnerships work

In this section, we will explore the role of school staff in partnerships between schools and community organisations.

School staff, including teachers, administrators, and support staff, play a critical role in the success of these partnerships. By engaging school staff in partnerships work, schools can tap into the expertise and resources of their staff and better support student learning and development. There are many ways that schools can engage school staff in partnerships work:

Involve staff in the planning process: Schools can involve staff in the planning and development of partnerships, allowing them to provide input and ideas about the initiatives and programs that will be most beneficial for students.

Provide professional development: Schools can offer professional development opportunities for staff to learn more about partnerships and how to effectively incorporate them into their work.

Encourage collaboration: Schools can encourage staff to collaborate with partners and share resources and expertise. This can help to create a sense of ownership and commitment to the partnership.

Recognise and reward staff contributions: Schools can recognise and reward the contributions of staff to partnerships, such as by providing opportunities for advancement or recognition in school newsletters or at school events.

By engaging school staff in partnerships work, schools can foster a culture of collaboration and innovation and better support student learning and development.

Implementation in real-world scenarios
Once again, the effectiveness of your approach depends on a multitude of factors. Consider how long your organisation has been involved in partnership activities, the level of familiarity your staff possesses regarding these activities, and whether any faculty members are actively engaged in them.

More questions arise than answers, as each organisation's solution will be tailored to its unique circumstances. However, a common thread runs through these considerations, which is the involvement of your staff in partnership work.

This doesn't necessarily mean that all staff members need to regularly welcome local children into their classrooms, but they should consistently hear about partnerships through various means. Providing a presentation each term detailing the ongoing initiatives, the individuals involved, and the impact on the community keeps everyone well-informed.

If your organisation has a shared staff area on its portal, maintaining a section that is regularly updated can be beneficial. Ensuring that the main social media channels frequently highlight partnership activities will keep staff members who follow these channels updated. Some schools even produce a weekly bulletin exclusively dedicated to partnerships or include a section in the headteacher's weekly bulletin. Thus, maintaining a steady stream of meaningful updates brings your staff along on the journey, even if they are not directly involved in the hands-on delivery. However, it is not solely about informing staff of your activities.

A significant aspect of this work revolves around winning 'hearts and minds.' Therefore, extra attention should be dedicated to developing your communication strategy to elucidate why this work is undertaken and how it enhances the education of students within your organisation, as well as those in partner schools.

This involves referencing the development of career knowledge, academic skills and knowledge, as well as those essential, albeit sometimes challenging to quantify, soft skills and future workplace skills.

Mastering the art of conveying this message and having a ready-made presentation at your disposal is valuable. Employing set phrases that you can use consistently, such as 'It's collaboration, not competition' or 'There is talent everywhere, but not opportunity,' can help you garner support without the need for extensive planning.

Most importantly, you must genuinely believe in the value of what you offer. A natural passion and a resolute commitment to enhancing the education of all children will shine through in your work if you genuinely hold these principles. If doubt exists, it may be worthwhile to reevaluate your strategy.

9: Staffing a partnerships department in a school

In this section, we will explore the importance of having a dedicated partnerships department in a school and how to effectively staff such a department.

A partnerships department is responsible for overseeing the partnerships that a school has with community organisations and ensuring that these collaborations are aligned with the school's goals and objectives.

There are a few key considerations when staffing a partnerships department in a school:

Identify key staff roles: It is important to identify the key staff roles that will be needed in the partnerships department, such as a partnerships coordinator or manager. These staff should have strong leadership skills, excellent communication skills, and the ability to build and maintain relationships.

Consider outside expertise: Schools may also want to consider bringing in outside expertise, such as consultants or advisors, to help with the planning and implementation of partnerships.

Involve other staff: While the partnerships department should have dedicated staff, it is important to involve other school staff in partnerships work as well. This can help to create a sense of ownership and commitment to the partnerships across the school.

By effectively staffing a partnerships department, schools can ensure that their partnerships are well-coordinated and aligned with the school's goals and objectives. This can help to maximise the benefits of partnerships for students and the school community.

Implementation in real-world scenarios

The allocation of staffing to partnership initiatives is often a nebulous challenge for organisations. It's not uncommon for schools to decide to establish a partnerships program and assign a few hours each week and a modest budget to make it happen.

Subsequently, they may assess the impact of more experienced practitioners across the UK and endeavour to replicate their success, often relying on evenings, weekends, and holidays to fill in the gaps.

When selecting staff for partnership work, it's crucial to maintain a sense of realism. Even seemingly straightforward events can demand a day's work in arranging transportation, conducting risk assessments, securing venues, addressing security and parking concerns, coordinating refreshments and meals, preparing surveys and evaluation materials, managing impact reporting tasks, engaging in ongoing email communication, handling medical records, catering and SEND (Special Educational Needs and Disabilities) requirements, and addressing other logistical aspects.

Organisations should initiate discussions regarding their partnership ambitions early on. They need to develop a comprehensive strategy, define their desired outcomes, and subsequently research the time and financial resources required to accomplish these tasks.

As previously discussed in preceding sections, networking and managing partner relationships entail significant work, so it's prudent to err on the side of overestimation rather than underestimation.

Given an appropriate level of time and funding, the next crucial step is to identify an individual with the requisite skills for the role. This person should be equally at ease in a classroom as they are in a boardroom, demonstrating a high level of motivation, enthusiasm, and excitement about the potential positive impact.

They should possess the ability to think creatively and challenge conventional norms, coupled with the confidence to approach both internal staff and external partners to drive initiatives forward.

A successful partnerships team member should also be a team player, capable of negotiating adeptly in the face of obstacles and resource constraints, such as venue availability and timetabling challenges.

Resilience is another vital trait for partnerships staff. They will frequently encounter obstacles that impede progress and confront the harsh realities experienced by disadvantaged individuals and communities. To excel in this role, they must be resourceful and receptive to alternative ideas, continuously striving to deliver the most impactful outcomes.

10: Engaging senior management and trustees in partnerships

In this section, we will explore the role of senior management and trustees in partnerships between schools and community organisations.

Senior management, including the principal and other school leaders, play a critical role in shaping the culture and direction of the school. Trustees, who are responsible for governing the school, also play a key role in supporting partnerships.

By engaging senior management and trustees in partnerships, schools can ensure that these collaborations align with the school's goals and objectives and have the support they need to be successful.

There are a few key strategies for engaging senior management and trustees in partnerships:

Communicate the value of partnerships: It is important to clearly communicate the value of partnerships to senior management and trustees. This can include highlighting the benefits for students, the school, and the community, as well as any data or research that supports the effectiveness of partnerships.

Involve them in the planning process: Schools can involve senior management and trustees in the planning and development of partnerships, allowing them to provide input and ideas about the initiatives and programs that will be most beneficial for the school.

Provide regular updates: Schools should provide regular updates to senior management and trustees about the progress and impact of partnerships. This can help to keep them informed and engaged.

By engaging senior management and trustees in partnerships, schools can ensure that these collaborations have the support and resources they need to be successful. This can help to maximise the benefits of partnerships for students and the school community.

Implementation in real-world scenarios
Engaging the senior team and the board is a paramount factor in the success of partnerships. These leaders should place this work at the core of their priorities and genuinely believe in the transformative potential it holds for enhancing the education of all children involved.

However, the degree to which this engagement is required may vary depending on your starting point and the existing support from the board. If there is not already unanimous support, your task is to convince them of the intrinsic value of partnerships to the broader community.

As with other facets of this endeavour, trust and proof of concept play pivotal roles. Delivering well-executed, smaller events and leveraging their benefits throughout the community can help win over those who may initially hold different perspectives.

Consistently offering high-quality activities will build a reputation for top-tier learning, complemented by positive feedback from the extended community.

Inevitably, conflicts may arise regarding the allocation of funds, whether for bursaries, scholarships, or partnership activities.

Similar disagreements may surface regarding capital investments or enhanced budgets for curriculum items. This is where your effective impact reporting, rooted in valuable data collected from all these initiatives, becomes invaluable. It enables you to make a compelling case for the value of partnership work.

You might discover instances where bursaries, scholarships, and partnerships intersect, with partner schools identifying ideal candidates for assistance. You could also find opportunities for partner schools to provide significant support in areas like Special Educational Needs and Disabilities (SEND) or the Arts, for example.

Even capital expenditures may align, as new facilities expand the resources available for sharing with partner schools and create more opportunities for the students involved.

Ensuring that the board actively participates in the initiatives and regularly engages in partnerships work is crucial. This firsthand involvement allows them to witness the inherent value and tangible benefits of these endeavours, solidifying their commitment to the journey.

11: Budgeting for partnerships

In this section, we will explore the importance of budgeting for partnerships between schools and community organisations. Effective budgeting is essential for ensuring that partnerships have the resources they need to be successful.

There are a few key considerations when budgeting for partnerships:

Identify the resources needed: It is important to identify the resources that will be needed for partnerships, such as staff time, materials, and financial resources. This will help to ensure that partnerships have the support they need to be successful.

Seek out external funding: Schools can seek out external funding sources, such as grants or donations, to support partnerships. This can help to offset the costs of partnerships and allow schools to do more with limited resources.

Involve partners in budgeting: Schools can involve partners in the budgeting process to ensure that the needs and priorities of both parties are taken into account.

Monitor and adjust: Schools should monitor the budget for partnerships and make adjustments as needed to ensure that resources are being used effectively.

By budgeting effectively for partnerships, schools can ensure that these collaborations have the resources they need to be successful and make a positive impact on student learning and development.

Implementation in real-world scenarios
Budgeting for partnerships can be a challenging endeavour, as the precise costs of a specific activity or initiative may remain elusive until you have executed it.

However, it's crucial to approach budget preparation for this work with a sense of realism. Even items such as staff time and venue costs, which may already be part of your organisation, should be included in your budget considerations.

You may have facilities such as a sports hall that is hired out commercially, so partnerships use would impact the income from that resource too. Conducting a thorough examination of each activity, from inception to conclusion, is a valuable task.

This includes accounting for factors such as email correspondence, travel expenses related to visiting partners, transportation costs for students and staff, and more. After you have organised a variety of events, you will gain a sense of the associated costs and become better equipped to submit accurate budget requests. Begin with smaller-scale initiatives and allocate a specific number of activities throughout the year. Over time, you'll learn the cost differences between hiring a coach and a minibus.

You'll delve into minibus light and mileage costs, become adept at crafting risk assessments, and familiarise yourself with catering charges for various types of lunches. You'll also amass knowledge about facilities, such as the seating capacity of rooms and the availability of fold-up tables stored in cupboards. Additionally, you'll compile lists of places to obtain more affordable resources. Once you have a few initial events under your belt, you can make more informed budget requests.

For instance, if you find that your staffing requirements consistently reach a particular threshold, you may conclude that this justifies hiring a part-time staff member at 0.5 FTE (Full-Time Equivalent), or even a full-time position. You can then benchmark the role through HR and incorporate the corresponding cost into your business case or proposal.

Partnerships is an area where you have the flexibility to scale your efforts up or down as needed and allocate resources accordingly. Naturally, your impact assessment will be applied to your expenditure to ensure that you are organising viable and meaningful events. You can adapt your strategies and resource allocation as you progress through the year.

Consequently, the initial ambition set by the board in the first year is based on estimated costs, followed by a more detailed proposal for the second year. To acquire realistic figures for events of a similar nature early in the process, consider reaching out to experienced partnerships leaders and requesting ballpark cost estimates.

While there may be unique 'wow' events that are one-offs in terms of budget, as you continue to build knowledge around the costs associated with various activities, you will become more adept at providing accurate estimations.

12: The importance of data analysis in partnerships

In this section, we will explore the role that data analysis plays in partnerships between schools and community organisations. Data analysis is the process of collecting, organising, and analysing data to understand trends, patterns, and relationships.

It is an essential part of partnerships because it allows schools and community organisations to understand the impact of their efforts and identify areas for improvement.

There are a few key considerations when it comes to data analysis in partnerships:

Identify the data that is needed: It is important to identify the data that will be needed to understand the impact of partnerships and to set goals and targets. This may include data about student outcomes, such as test scores and attendance rates, as well as data about the partnerships themselves, such as participation rates and feedback from stakeholders.

Collect data in a systematic way: Schools and community organisations should collect data in a systematic way to ensure that it is accurate and reliable. This may involve using tools such as surveys, focus groups, or observations.

Analyse the data: Once data has been collected, it is important to analyse it to understand trends, patterns, and relationships. Schools and community organisations can use a variety of tools and techniques, such as statistical analysis or visualisations, to help make sense of the data.

Use the data to inform decisions: The final step in the data analysis process is to use the insights from the data to inform decisions about partnerships. Schools and community organisations can use the data to set goals, identify areas for improvement, and make adjustments to their partnerships as needed.

By engaging in data analysis, schools and community organisations can better understand the impact of their partnerships and use this information to improve student learning and development.

Implementation in real-world scenarios

The quality of your data analysis is fundamentally dependent on the data you collect in the first place. Therefore, acquiring the right data is equally as important as the analysis itself.

High-quality data is not only easy to collect but also readily interpretable, especially when it is structured in a format conducive to easy querying. While the specifics of data types will be discussed elsewhere in this book, it's crucial to contemplate how you will utilise the data and interpret it in relation to your Key Performance Indicators (KPIs) and desired outcomes.

Once you've identified the data you need, the questions you ask become equally vital. You'll aim to gather both quantitative and qualitative data. Historically, quantitative data was simpler to interpret and derive meaningful evaluations from, while qualitative data presented challenges in terms of analysis. Comments or survey responses provided valuable testimonials for websites and invaluable feedback for refining your offerings, but analysing extensive volumes of feedback forms could be daunting.

Fortunately, with the advent of Artificial Intelligence (AI), we can now upload our feedback data and request AI systems to summarise the content into concise bullet points. It's even possible to assign metrics to text and extract quantifiable insights. However, relying solely on AI should not comprise the entire impact assessment, as computers may miss subtleties in the data. Therefore, some manual analysis will still be necessary.

Impact assessment data serves two crucial purposes: informing us about our performance and holding us accountable for the work we undertake. By capturing data related to factors such as age, gender, demographics, timing, financial costs, subject disciplines, and curriculum areas, you can swiftly evaluate how well you are meeting specific criteria.

For example, you might discover that your focus leans heavily towards local partnerships and neglects international ones, or that you are more active with Key Stage 1 (KS1) than Key Stage 4 (KS4). You may realise that a disproportionate amount of resources is allocated to one subject area.

Having data stored in an organised manner enables you to query it post-collection as well. If a board member raises a specific question, you can investigate the data in a novel way to obtain the answer. It is vital to remember that data is rarely perfect. While it is a coveted asset in partnerships work, it can be open to various interpretations. Consistency in your analysis is essential.

13: Change management in partnerships

In this section, we will explore the role of change management in partnerships between schools and community organisations.

Change management refers to the process of planning, implementing, and communicating changes to partnerships in a way that minimises disruption and maximises the chances of success.

Effective change management is essential for partnerships because it helps to ensure that changes are implemented smoothly and that all stakeholders are aware of and supportive of the changes.

There are a few key considerations when it comes to change management in partnerships:

Establish clear goals and objectives: It is important to establish clear goals and objectives for the changes being made to partnerships. This will help to ensure that everyone is aligned and working towards the same goals.

Communicate with stakeholders: Schools and community organisations should communicate with stakeholders about the changes being made to partnerships. This can help to build support and understanding for the changes and minimise disruption.

Provide training and support: Schools and community organisations should provide training and support as needed to help stakeholders adapt to the changes. This may involve providing resources, guidance, or professional development opportunities.

Monitor and adjust: Schools and community organisations should monitor the changes being made to partnerships and make adjustments as needed to ensure that they are successful.

By effectively managing change, schools and community organisations can minimise disruption and maximise the chances of success for their partnerships. This can help to ensure that partnerships continue to support student learning and development over time.

Implementation in real-world scenarios

Change management is a pivotal aspect of effective partnership initiatives, and its success hinges on meticulous planning and execution. The ability to manage change efficiently can significantly influence the outcomes and sustainability of collaborative efforts.

This critical process can vary in complexity, depending on the nature of the partnership and its objectives. The first step in effective change management within partnerships is understanding the necessity for change.

Partners must collectively identify the areas that require modification, whether it's refining the partnership's goals, restructuring operational processes, or adapting to evolving circumstances.

Clear communication among stakeholders is paramount at this stage, fostering shared understanding and commitment to change. Once the need for change is established, a well-defined strategy must be developed. This strategy outlines the specific changes, their goals, and the timeline for implementation.

Collaboration is key during this phase, as partners must work together to craft a comprehensive plan that accommodates all stakeholders' perspectives and concerns.

Change management also entails creating an environment conducive to change. This involves garnering support from leadership teams and ensuring that they endorse the proposed changes. Leaders must demonstrate commitment to the partnership's evolution, inspiring confidence in their teams.

Open and transparent communication channels should be established to address questions, concerns, and feedback from all stakeholders. Effective change management relies heavily on engaging and involving those directly impacted by the changes. This includes staff, students, and any other relevant parties.

Engaging stakeholders fosters a sense of ownership and accountability, reducing resistance to change. Regular updates, training sessions, and workshops can facilitate this process, ensuring that everyone is equipped to adapt to the new landscape.

Monitoring and evaluating the progress of change initiatives is essential. This involves collecting data and feedback to assess whether the desired outcomes are being achieved. Adjustments may be necessary along the way to fine-tune the approach and ensure alignment with the partnership's objectives.

Change management in partnerships is a multifaceted process that demands careful planning, effective communication, and collaboration among all stakeholders. When executed thoughtfully, it can lead to positive transformations, improved outcomes, and the sustained success of collaborative endeavours.

This may involve identifying ways to streamline processes, reduce waste, or leverage resources from other partners. By effectively managing resources, schools and community organisations can maximise the chances of success for their partnerships and better support student learning and development.

14: Resource management in partnerships

In this section, we will explore the role of resource management in partnerships between schools and community organisations. Resource management refers to the process of planning, allocating, and utilising resources in a way that maximises the chances of success for partnerships.

Effective resource management is essential for partnerships because it helps to ensure that partnerships have the resources, they need to be successful.

There are a few key considerations when it comes to resource management in partnerships:

Identify the resources needed: It is important to identify the resources that will be needed for partnerships, such as staff time, materials, and financial resources. This will help to ensure that partnerships have the support they need to be successful.

Allocate resources effectively: Schools and community organisations should allocate resources effectively to ensure that they are being used in the most efficient and effective way possible. This may involve prioritising certain initiatives or programs, or identifying ways to stretch resources further.

Utilise resources efficiently: Schools and community organisations should also utilise resources efficiently to ensure that they are getting the most value for their investment. This may involve identifying ways to streamline processes, reduce waste, or leverage resources from other partners.

By effectively managing resources, schools and community organisations can maximise the chances of success for their partnerships and better support student learning and development.

Implementation in real-world scenarios

Resource management in partnerships work is a complex endeavour, encompassing a wide array of assets and opportunities. To effectively manage these resources, it is essential to understand the various elements that contribute to the success of collaborative initiatives.

First and foremost, defining what constitutes a resource in the context of partnerships is crucial. These resources can range from tangible assets like science labs, swimming pools, tennis courts, forests, football pitches, and theatres to intangible resources like academic staff expertise, financial support, human resources, and educational strategies. Financial resources, in particular, play a significant role in enabling partnerships work, as they provide the necessary funds to implement collaborative activities.

One key principle of resource management in partnerships is the recognition of shared resources and the importance of mutuality. Rather than viewing resources as exclusive to one partner, it should be a matter of coordinating and scheduling their use.

This approach fosters a sense of equity and collaboration, moving away from the 'we do unto them' mentality that sometimes plagues independent-state school partnerships. Practical resource sharing can take various forms, such as sharing personnel across partner schools or providing direct access to booking forms for shared resources.

However, careful consideration must be given to the potential demands and limitations of these resources. For instance, a resource may already be in use by students at a particular school during certain times of the week, or a teacher may have a full timetable, making them unavailable for additional commitments.

Additionally, some resources may have financial expectations tied to their use and diverting them for partnerships purposes could impact revenue generation. To effectively manage resources, it is advisable to conduct a comprehensive resource audit, identifying available assets and assessing their accessibility for partnerships. This audit should also include an analysis of how to leverage these resources to maximise their utility and impact. Moreover, sustainability should be a paramount consideration, encompassing environmental concerns, community engagement, and long-term viability.

15: Building relationships with local schools

In this section, we will explore the importance of building relationships with local schools and the role that these relationships can play in supporting student learning and development.

Building relationships with local schools can help to create a sense of community and collaboration among schools and can provide opportunities for students to learn and grow.

There are a few key strategies for building relationships with local schools:

Reach out to local schools: Schools can reach out to other schools in the community to explore potential partnerships. This may involve contacting school leaders or teachers, attending local education events, or participating in local education organisations.

Collaborate on initiatives and programs: Schools can collaborate on initiatives and programs that benefit students and the larger community. This may involve sharing resources, expertise, or facilities, or working together on community service projects.

Share best practices: Schools can share best practices and ideas with each other to improve student learning and development. This may involve hosting professional development opportunities or sharing resources and materials.

Engage in joint planning: Schools can engage in joint planning to align their efforts and ensure that they are working towards common goals. This may involve creating a collaborative planning committee or establishing regular meetings to discuss shared goals and objectives.

By building relationships with local schools, schools can create a sense of community and collaboration and better support student learning and development.

Implementation in real-world scenarios

The dynamics of building and managing partnerships often revolve around the pre-existing relationships among schools and organisations involved, as well as the collective experiences of stakeholders.

Successfully navigating this terrain requires a genuine and authentic approach focused on enhancing educational outcomes for all children involved. Initiating potential partnerships with other schools should be driven by a sincere commitment to improving education and fostering a positive environment for shared responsibilities.

When this genuine intention is at the forefront, conversations tend to be positive and fruitful, laying the groundwork for collaborative efforts in the future.

Conducting research in the local area to identify existing partnerships among schools and discerning which schools are part of a Trust/Multi-Academy Trust (MAT) or a similar formal association is essential.

It is often easier for a secondary school to collaborate with a primary school, and vice versa, given the natural progression of educational stages. However, potential conflicts of interest may arise when a prep school interacts with primary or secondary schools within the same key stages.

While collaboration should always be the guiding principle over competition, schools must consider the possibility that parents may choose to relocate their children if they perceive another organisation to offer a superior educational experience. This emphasis on enrolment can sometimes lead to tensions between schools.

Building strong relationships with senior leaders, office staff, and teachers at other schools is pivotal in uncovering opportunities for collaboration.

Establishing informal channels of communication, such as a 'WhatsApp relationship,' where peers can engage in relaxed conversations without the need for formal emails and paperwork, fosters a more open and productive dialogue. Some partnership groups may require schools to pay for membership, adding an additional layer of negotiation concerning the perceived value for money.

It is important to ensure that all schools in the area, regardless of their financial capacity, have the opportunity to participate. Often, those schools that stand to benefit the most from collaborative efforts may be less inclined to reach out and more defensive when approached. Inclusivity is paramount, and financial constraints should not exclude any school from participating.

Ultimately, creating an atmosphere where stakeholders feel comfortable and at ease with each other increases the likelihood of ongoing interaction and the discovery of opportunities that benefit the children in their care.

A lot of partnerships meet once or twice a term to network, meet face to face and discuss trends in education and make future plans.

16: Crowdfunding

Crowdfunding is a method of raising funds for a project or activity by soliciting small contributions from a large number of people, typically via the internet. It has become a popular way for individuals, organisations, and businesses to raise money for various projects and initiatives, including school partnerships activities.

One of the key benefits of crowdfunding for school partnerships activities is that it allows schools to tap into a wider pool of potential donors. This can be particularly useful for schools that are looking to raise funds for a specific project or activity, such as a school-to-school partnership program.

Another benefit of crowdfunding for school partnerships activities is that it can be a relatively low-cost way to raise funds. With many crowdfunding platforms, there are no up-front costs for creating a campaign, and the platform takes a small percentage of the funds raised as a fee. When it comes to school partnerships activities, crowdfunding can be used to raise funds for a variety of initiatives such as:

- Travel expenses for students and staff to visit partner schools materials and equipment for collaborative projects or activities
- Professional development for teachers to support the partnership
- Cultural exchange programs

To run a successful crowdfunding campaign for school partnerships activities, it's important to have a clear and compelling story to tell. The campaign should include a detailed description of the partnership and its goals, as well as information about how the funds raised will be used. It's also important to have a clear and achievable funding goal, and to promote the campaign widely to potential donors.

Implementation in real-world scenarios
Crowdfunding for school partnerships activities is a dynamic and evolving approach that requires careful planning and execution.

Much like partnerships themselves, the success of crowdfunding campaigns can be influenced by the relationships that schools have cultivated within their communities, the level of engagement from stakeholders, and the shared vision for enhancing education.

Starting a crowdfunding campaign for partnerships activities often begins with a clear and compelling message that resonates with potential supporters. This message should emphasise the mutual benefits of partnerships for both the school and the broader community, highlighting the positive impact on education and the students involved.

Prior research into the local community and its interests is invaluable. Identifying individuals or groups who are passionate about education and open to supporting collaborative initiatives can make a significant difference.

This could include parents, alumni, local businesses, and even other schools that have successfully implemented partnerships. Engagement is key. Schools should actively involve their stakeholders, including students, parents, teachers, and alumni, in the crowdfunding process.

This can be achieved through effective communication, utilising various channels like social media, newsletters, and school events to create awareness and encourage contributions. Personalised messages that emphasise the collective effort and the tangible benefits of partnerships are often more persuasive.

Crowdfunding platforms provide a convenient way to manage and track contributions. Schools should select a platform that aligns with their goals and allows for easy sharing of campaign updates and progress. Setting a realistic fundraising target is crucial, and it should be accompanied by a detailed breakdown of how the funds will be used for partnerships activities.

Incentives and rewards can be powerful motivators. Offering donors recognition, exclusive access to partnership events, or other meaningful acknowledgments can encourage more substantial contributions. The goal is not only to raise funds but also to strengthen the sense of community and ownership over the partnerships initiative.

17: Partnerships in schools and service learning

In this section, we will explore the relationship between partnerships in schools and service learning.

Service learning is a teaching and learning approach that combines academic coursework with meaningful service to the community. Service learning can be a powerful tool for enhancing student learning and development, and partnerships with community organisations can play a key role in supporting service-learning initiatives.

There are a few key ways in which partnerships in schools and service learning can work together:

Partnerships can provide opportunities for service learning: Schools can partner with community organisations to provide opportunities for students to engage in service learning. This may involve working with organisations that provide services to the community, such as hospitals, shelters, or environmental organisations.

Service learning can enhance partnerships: Service learning can also enhance partnerships between schools and community organisations by providing a way for students to actively contribute to and learn from the partnerships. This can help to create a sense of ownership and commitment to the partnerships among students.

Partnerships can support service-learning initiatives:
Schools can leverage partnerships to support service learning initiatives by seeking out funding, resources, and expertise from community organisations. This can help to ensure that service-learning initiatives have the support they need to be successful.

By leveraging partnerships in schools and service learning, schools can enhance student learning and development and make a positive impact on the community.

Implementation in real-world scenarios
Service learning and partnerships represent a unique opportunity for schools to create a symbiotic relationship that benefits both students and the broader community. It's essential to recognise that service learning should not be a one-way street but should be integrated into partnerships in a mutually beneficial manner.

Many elements of the curriculum inherently involve service, such as the International Baccalaureate's core component, "Service and action," the Duke of Edinburgh Award, MYP projects, and various subjects like Design and Technology and PSHE.

These avenues provide students with opportunities to engage in service activities that enrich their learning experience. Service learning can take many forms, from older students serving as role models or mentors to younger ones, to students with English as a second language assisting in language classes.

They can also raise funds for educational activities, spend time in care homes interacting with residents, volunteer for charities like riding for the disabled or charity shops, and engage with numerous third-party organisations. Partnerships with these external entities are crucial for facilitating such service opportunities across schools.

One of the significant benefits of service learning within partnerships is the chance to take students out of their comfort zones and immerse them in new environments. This exposure is instrumental in preparing them for the future workplace, as they acquire valuable skills and enhance their interpersonal abilities. Students gain insights into different demographics, cultures, and perspectives, potentially challenging and broadening their worldviews.

While it's possible to pursue partnerships without directly linking them to the service curriculum, combining the two provides an easy win. By integrating service learning into partnerships, all partner schools offer their students the chance to engage in meaningful and impactful activities while simultaneously enhancing their learning experiences.

Of course, there are logistical challenges to overcome, such as addressing safeguarding concerns and organising transportation. However, the value created by these integrated partnerships far outweighs the barriers, making it a worthwhile endeavour for both students and the community they serve.

18: Local, national, and international partnerships

In this section, we will explore the different types of partnerships that schools can engage in and the benefits of each type. Schools can engage in partnerships at the local, national, and international level, and each type of partnership has its own unique benefits and challenges.

Local partnerships involve collaborations with organisations or institutions within the same community as the school. These partnerships can provide opportunities for students to learn about and engage with their local community and can help to create a sense of community and collaboration among schools and organisations.

National partnerships involve collaborations with organisations or institutions from across the country. These partnerships can provide opportunities for students to learn about and engage with a wider range of perspectives and experiences and can help to broaden their understanding of the world.

International partnerships involve collaborations with organisations or institutions from other countries. These partnerships can provide opportunities for students to learn about and engage with different cultures and ways of life and can help to foster a sense of global citizenship.

By engaging in partnerships at the local, national, and international level, schools can provide students with a range of learning opportunities and help to broaden their understanding of the world.

Implementation in real-world scenarios
The approach to partnerships in terms of locality, national reach, and international engagement varies significantly based on the specific context of each school. Whether a school is a prep/primary, middle school, or secondary, and its size and demographic makeup, all influence its priorities in this realm.

Many schools cultivate international links through projects aimed at supporting communities with limited access to education resources. These initiatives often involve trips to countries for teaching or building projects, as well as regular video conferencing to connect communities and foster cultural exchange.

It is evident that focusing solely on international impact could lead to overlooking local and national needs, despite the potentially greater impact and cost-effectiveness of initiatives in deprived areas abroad. For instance, projects like restoring a child's eyesight for £20 or installing renewable energy in African villages have transformative effects.

However, it's crucial to offer partnerships across all three levels—local, national, and international—to enrich the education of all students involved. To prevent partnerships from becoming mere acts of "charity tourism," schools should foster meaningful connections through ongoing engagement, such as pen pal schemes or weekly video conferencing sessions.

This approach ensures that interactions between schools are not isolated events but rather ongoing exchanges that promote understanding and collaboration. Engaging with children from diverse regions, demographics, and cultures is essential for developing global citizenship among students.

Establishing substantial links between independent and international schools, which can then be shared with partner primary schools, facilitates regular interaction with minimal administrative burden.

Measuring the impact of these partnerships poses an interesting challenge. When organising trips abroad, schools must consider their carbon footprint and ensure that any expertise or resources brought to the country are genuinely needed.

It is crucial to evaluate whether a trip serves a significant educational purpose or is merely a well-intentioned gesture.

19: Maintaining relationships in partnerships
In this section, we will explore the importance of maintaining relationships in partnerships between schools and community organisations. Maintaining relationships is essential for partnerships because it helps to ensure that partnerships continue to thrive and have a positive impact on student learning and development.

There are a few key strategies for maintaining relationships in partnerships:

Foster open communication: It is important to foster open communication between schools and community organisations to ensure that partnerships are meeting the needs of all stakeholders. This may involve establishing regular communication channels, such as meetings or newsletters, or using tools such as surveys to gather feedback.

Foster a sense of collaboration: Schools and community organisations should work to foster a sense of collaboration and mutual support in partnerships. This may involve sharing resources, expertise, or facilities, or working together on initiatives and programs.

Foster a sense of ownership: Schools and community organisations should work to foster a sense of ownership and commitment to partnerships among all stakeholders. This may involve students, teachers, and other community members in the planning and implementation of partnerships.

By maintaining relationships in partnerships, schools and community organisations can ensure that partnerships continue to thrive and have a positive impact on student learning and development.

Implementation in real-world scenarios

Effective communication and relationship management are often overlooked aspects of partnership planning but are crucial for success. The strength of connections between lead individuals from each organisation is paramount.

A robust partnership thrives when these individuals know each other well and feel comfortable navigating difficult conversations when necessary. Relationships will inevitably face challenges, but regular communication between counterparts is essential to maintain effectiveness. The mode of communication may vary depending on organisational culture and individual preferences. Some leaders may prefer digital channels like WhatsApp or email, while others may opt for face-to-face meetings over coffee.

For partnerships involving three or more organisations, scheduling formal gatherings as part of the working day ensures dedicated time for discussing concerns and sharing ideas in a safe space. In addition to formal meetings, informal gatherings such as lunches or dinners provide opportunities for partnership leads to strengthen bonds on a personal level.

Transparent and open communication fosters a sense of belonging among stakeholders, enabling them to suggest innovative ideas or address issues openly. Flexibility and understanding are key when it comes to managing time constraints and unforeseen circumstances.

Supporting colleagues during busy periods or personal challenges demonstrates empathy and reinforces the collaborative spirit essential for successful partnerships.

Ultimately, these relationships are the foundation of effective partnerships. Investing time and resources in nurturing them should be prioritised, as they form the backbone of any successful collaborative endeavour.

20: Ensuring that budgets in partnerships are spent on those with the most need

In this section, we will explore the importance of ensuring that budgets in partnerships between schools and community organisations are spent on those with the most need. Ensuring that budgets are spent equitably is essential for partnerships because it helps to ensure that resources are being used to support the students and communities that need them the most.

There are a few key strategies for ensuring that budgets in partnerships are spent on those with the most need:

Identify the needs of the community: It is important to identify the needs of the community served by partnerships to ensure that resources are being used effectively. This may involve conducting needs assessments or gathering input from community members.

Allocate resources based on need: Schools and community organisations should allocate resources based on the needs of the community. This may involve prioritising certain initiatives or programs, or allocating resources in a way that ensures that they are reaching those with the most need.

Monitor and adjust: Schools and community organisations should regularly monitor the impact of their partnerships and make adjustments as needed to ensure that resources are being used effectively. This may involve collecting data about student outcomes or gathering feedback from community members.

By ensuring that budgets in partnerships are spent on those with the most need, schools and community organisations can better support student learning and development and make a positive impact on the community.

Implementation in real-world scenarios

Addressing the diverse needs of all students within a partnership framework is a multifaceted endeavour. While special educational needs and socioeconomic disadvantage are commonly acknowledged, it's important to recognise that every child, regardless of background, may have unique needs.

Partnerships should strive to enhance the educational experience for all students across the network of schools involved. This may involve organising events specifically tailored to support students with special educational needs, while also incorporating participation from peers in other schools to foster understanding and empathy. Exposing students to different realities beyond their own is crucial for fostering empathy and understanding.

Wealthy families may face their own challenges, such as absence of parental role models or siblings with disabilities. Therefore, budget allocation in partnerships should not solely focus on traditional metrics like free school meals or pupil premium but should also consider other hidden needs within the student body.

Open discussions involving schools, teachers, parents, and students, along with feedback mechanisms like surveys and data analysis, are essential for identifying and addressing these diverse needs effectively. Embracing criticism and demonstrating a willingness to adapt based on community feedback is integral to creating an inclusive educational environment that supports the mental health and well-being of all students, irrespective of their backgrounds.

21: Sustaining partnerships

In this section, we will explore the importance of sustaining partnerships between schools and community organisations. Sustaining partnerships is essential for ensuring that they continue to have a positive impact on student learning and development over time.

There are a few key strategies for sustaining partnerships:

Foster a sense of commitment: Schools and community organisations should work to foster a sense of commitment to partnerships among all stakeholders. This may involve students, teachers, and other community members in the planning and implementation of partnerships or creating a sense of ownership and responsibility for the partnerships.

Foster open communication: It is important to foster open communication between schools and community organisations to ensure that partnerships are meeting the needs of all stakeholders. This may involve establishing regular communication channels, such as meetings or newsletters, or using tools such as surveys to gather feedback.

Monitor and adjust: Schools and community organisations should regularly monitor the impact of their partnerships and make adjustments as needed to ensure that they are meeting the needs of all stakeholders and having a positive impact on student learning and development.

By sustaining partnerships, schools and community organisations can ensure that they continue to have a positive impact on student learning and development over time.

Implementation in real-world scenarios

Ensuring continuity and effective succession planning within partnership leadership is paramount for the longevity and success of collaborative efforts in schools. It's common for turnover to occur in leadership positions, whether due to staff moving to other roles, or schools or shifts in responsibilities.

Succession planning involves preparing for these changes by providing shadowing opportunities for incoming leads, allowing for a smooth transition of relationships and procedures. Since each individual brings their unique personality and approach to the role, the transition can sometimes strain existing relationships if not managed carefully.

Having multiple staff members involved in partnership activities can naturally mitigate succession challenges, as relationships are shared, reducing the risk of simultaneous departures and facilitating seamless transitions.

Financial stability is another crucial factor in sustaining partnership initiatives. External factors such as pandemics, global conflicts, or shifts in educational policies can impact the availability of funds. Schools may face challenges in affording teacher cover, transportation, or other associated costs, potentially jeopardising the continuity of programs. It's essential to anticipate these challenges and incorporate sustainability measures into partnership planning.

Each event or initiative should undergo due diligence to ensure it is sustainable in the long term. This includes outlining clear exit strategies for repeatable programs and safeguarding against potential disruptions in funding or support.

Additionally, partnerships should avoid creating dependency among participating communities, particularly in international collaborations, to mitigate risks associated with fluctuating support levels.

By proactively addressing these factors, partnerships can enhance their resilience and long-term impact.

22: Communicating with different stakeholders in partnerships

In this section, we will explore the importance of good communication in partnerships between schools and community organisations and how to effectively communicate with different stakeholders.

Effective communication is essential for partnerships

because it helps to ensure that all stakeholders are aware of and supportive of the partnerships.

There are a few key strategies for communicating with different stakeholders in partnerships:

Identify the stakeholders: It is important to identify all of the stakeholders in partnerships, including students, teachers, parents, community members, and other organisations.

Determine the best communication channels: Schools and community organisations should determine the best communication channels for reaching each stakeholder group. This may involve using a combination of methods, such as newsletters, meetings, social media, or email.

Customise the message: Schools and community organisations should tailor the message to the specific needs and interests of each stakeholder group. This may involve providing different types of information or using different language and tone.

Engage in two-way communication: Schools and community organisations should engage in two-way communication with stakeholders to ensure that they are receiving feedback and addressing any concerns. This may involve hosting meetings or focus groups or using tools such as surveys to gather input.

By effectively communicating with different stakeholders in partnerships, schools and community organisations can ensure that all stakeholders are aware of and supportive of the partnerships.

Implementation in real-world scenarios

Effective communication with various stakeholders is fundamental to the success of partnership initiatives in schools. Each stakeholder group, whether it's teachers, parents, students, or external partners, plays a crucial role in the collaborative effort and must be engaged appropriately.

Teachers: Keeping educators informed and involved is essential as they are often directly involved in implementing partnership activities. Regular updates through staff meetings, newsletters, or dedicated communication channels ensure that teachers understand the objectives, benefits, and logistics of partnership projects. Providing opportunities for feedback and input encourages teacher engagement and ownership of the initiatives.

Parents: Engaging parents in partnership activities fosters community support and involvement. Communication avenues such as parent newsletters, information sessions, and parent-teacher meetings can be utilised to share updates on partnership projects, solicit feedback, and encourage parental participation. Clear communication about the goals and outcomes of partnerships helps parents understand the value of these initiatives for their children's education and personal development.

Students: Involving students in the communication process empowers them to take ownership of partnership activities and fosters a sense of responsibility. Utilising student councils, assemblies, and classroom discussions to share information about upcoming projects and opportunities allows students to voice their opinions, express interests, and contribute ideas. Transparent communication helps students understand the purpose and impact of partnerships on their learning experience.

External Partners: Building strong relationships with external partners requires effective communication and collaboration. Regular meetings, email updates, and progress reports keep partners informed about project developments, milestones, and challenges. Clarifying roles, expectations, and responsibilities ensures alignment and fosters a sense of shared purpose. Open channels of communication enable partners to provide feedback, share resources, and address issues collaboratively.

Community: Communicating partnership initiatives to the broader community enhances transparency and generates support. Utilising school websites, social media platforms, and local newspapers to showcase partnership activities, successes, and testimonials highlights the positive impact on the community.

Engaging community members through events, volunteer opportunities, and public forums fosters a sense of pride and ownership in the collaborative efforts.

Leadership: Keeping school leadership informed and engaged is critical for securing ongoing support and resources for partnership initiatives. Regular updates, presentations, and progress reports demonstrate the value and impact of partnerships on educational outcomes and school culture.

Engaging leaders in strategic discussions and decision-making processes ensures alignment with organisational goals and priorities. By tailoring communication strategies to the specific needs and preferences of each stakeholder group, schools can cultivate a culture of collaboration, transparency, and shared ownership in partnership endeavours.

Effective communication strengthens relationships, builds trust, and maximizes the collective impact of collaborative efforts.

23: Planning a framework for partnerships

In this section, we will explore the process of planning a framework for partnerships between schools and community organisations.

A framework is a set of guiding principles and practices that helps to define the goals and objectives of partnerships, as well as the roles and responsibilities of all stakeholders.

There are a few key steps in planning a framework for partnerships:

Identify the goals and objectives of the partnerships: It is important to identify the goals and objectives of the partnerships to ensure that they are aligned with the needs and priorities of all stakeholders. This may involve engaging in needs assessments or gathering input from students, teachers, and community members.

Determine the roles and responsibilities of all stakeholders: Schools and community organisations should determine the roles and responsibilities of all stakeholders in the partnerships. This may involve identifying who will be responsible for planning and implementing initiatives, who will be responsible for managing resources, and who will be responsible for monitoring and evaluating the impact of the partnerships.

Develop a plan for implementing the partnerships: Schools and community organisations should develop a detailed plan for implementing the partnerships, including a timeline, budget, and action steps. This plan should be shared with all stakeholders and should be regularly reviewed and updated as needed.

By planning a framework for partnerships, schools and community organisations can ensure that partnerships are aligned with the needs and priorities of all stakeholders and are implemented in a way that is effective and efficient.

Implementation in real-world scenarios
Planning a framework for partnerships requires a systematic approach to ensure effectiveness and sustainability.

As discussed in previous sections, it's crucial to start with thorough research and develop a comprehensive strategy. This involves identifying potential partner organisations, understanding community needs, assessing available resources, and analysing best practices in collaborative initiatives.

Building on this research, a robust strategy should be developed in collaboration with colleagues from partner organisations, articulating a theory of change and establishing clear and measurable outcomes. Once the strategy is in place, it's essential to establish policies and procedures for various aspects of the partnerships program. This includes protocols for data collection and impact reporting, transport arrangements, risk assessment and safeguarding procedures.

A collaborative framework should also be established to clarify roles, responsibilities, and expectations for all stakeholders, fostering transparency, accountability, and trust.

Investing in capacity building is essential for empowering stakeholders to effectively participate in partnership initiatives. This may involve providing training and professional development opportunities to enhance skills in project management, communication, and cultural competency.

Additionally, fostering a culture of continuous improvement is crucial, allowing for ongoing reflection, learning, and adaptation based on feedback and changing circumstances. By following this systematic approach and engaging stakeholders throughout the process, schools can create impactful and sustainable partnerships that benefit the entire community.

24: Dealing with community members who oppose partnerships

In this section, we will explore strategies for dealing with community members who oppose partnerships between schools and community organisations.
It is not uncommon for partnerships to face opposition from some members of the community, and it is important for schools and community organisations to have strategies in place for addressing these concerns.

There are a few key strategies for dealing with community members who oppose partnerships:

Engage in dialogue: It is important to engage in dialogue with community members who oppose partnerships to understand their concerns and address them. This may involve hosting meetings or focus groups or using tools such as surveys to gather input.

Communicate the benefits of the partnerships: Schools and community organisations should communicate the benefits of the partnerships to community members who oppose them. This may involve sharing data about the impact of the partnerships on student learning and development or sharing testimonials from students, teachers, and other stakeholders.

Address concerns and address conflicts: Schools and community organisations should work to address any concerns or conflicts that arise in partnerships in a constructive way. This may involve seeking mediation or working with a third party to resolve conflicts. By dealing with community members who oppose partnerships in a proactive and constructive way, schools and community organisations can build support for the partnerships and ensure that they have a positive impact on student learning and development.

Implementation in real-world scenarios

Dealing with community members who oppose partnerships requires a proactive and empathetic approach to address concerns and foster understanding. It is essential to start by listening to the reasons behind their opposition and acknowledging their perspectives respectfully. This demonstrates empathy and opens the door for constructive dialogue.

Communication plays a crucial role in addressing opposition.

Schools should engage in transparent and open communication with community members, providing clear and accurate information about the purpose and benefits of partnerships. This may involve organising community forums, distributing informational materials, and utilising various communication channels to reach a wide audience.

Educating the community about the positive impacts of partnerships is key to overcoming opposition. Schools can highlight success stories, testimonials, and data demonstrating the tangible benefits of collaboration, such as improved educational outcomes, enhanced community engagement, and increased access to resources and opportunities.

Addressing misconceptions and dispelling myths is also important in addressing opposition. Schools should provide information to counter misinformation and clarify any misunderstandings about the nature and goals of partnerships. Engaging in honest and transparent dialogue helps build trust and credibility with community members.

Furthermore, involving community members in the partnership process can help alleviate concerns and foster a sense of ownership and investment in the initiatives. Schools can invite community members to participate in planning committees, advisory boards, and community engagement activities, empowering them to contribute their ideas and perspectives.

Finally, it's crucial to remain patient, resilient, and committed to addressing opposition over the long term. Change often takes time, and building consensus and support for partnerships may require ongoing efforts to engage with community members, address concerns, and demonstrate the value of collaboration for the greater good of the community.

25: Explaining the involvement of independent schools in partnerships to the community

In this section, we will explore strategies for explaining the involvement of independent schools in partnerships to the community. Independent schools are private schools that are not affiliated with a particular religion or government agency, and they may have different motivations for engaging in partnerships than public schools.

It is important for independent schools to communicate their reasons for participating in partnerships to the community in a clear and transparent way.

There are a few key strategies for explaining the involvement of independent schools in partnerships to the community:

Communicate the goals and objectives of the partnerships: It is important for independent schools to communicate the goals and objectives of the partnerships to the community in a clear and concise way. This may involve sharing data about the impact of the partnerships on student learning and development or describing the specific initiatives and programs that are being implemented.

Share the benefits of the partnerships: Independent schools should share the benefits of the partnerships with the community, including how the partnerships are supporting student learning and development and benefiting the community as a whole.

Engage in dialogue: Independent schools should engage in dialogue with community members to answer questions and address concerns about the partnerships. This may involve hosting meetings or focus groups or using tools such as surveys to gather input.

By explaining the involvement of independent schools in partnerships to the community in a clear and transparent way, independent schools can build support for the partnerships and ensure that they have a positive impact on student learning and development.

Implementation in real-world scenarios
Explaining the involvement of schools in partnerships to the community requires a thoughtful and comprehensive approach aimed at fostering understanding and garnering support. It begins with transparent communication channels and a commitment to addressing community concerns with empathy and respect.

Schools prioritise clear and open communication to convey the purpose, benefits, and objectives of partnerships to the community. Through various platforms such as community meetings, newsletters, and social media, schools disseminate accurate information about their collaborative efforts, highlighting the positive impacts on students, educators, and the broader community.

Educating the community about the significance of partnerships is essential in gaining community support.

Schools must share success stories and testimonials that illustrate the tangible benefits of collaboration, including enhanced educational opportunities, increased access to resources, and strengthened community ties. Addressing misconceptions and clarifying any misunderstandings is crucial in building community trust.

Schools should provide factual information to counter misinformation and offer transparent explanations of partnership initiatives, ensuring that community members have accurate insights into the nature and goals of these collaborations. Involving the community in the partnership process fosters a sense of ownership and investment.

Schools should invite community members to participate in planning committees, advisory boards, and collaborative projects, empowering them to contribute their ideas and perspectives to partnership activities.

Persistence and commitment are key in navigating community perceptions and building support for partnerships over time. By maintaining open lines of communication, actively engaging with community concerns, and demonstrating the positive outcomes of collaboration, schools can effectively explain their involvement in partnerships and garner community support for their initiatives.

26: Charitable status and the use of charitable funding for partnerships

In this section, we will explore the relationship between charitable status and the use of charitable funding for partnerships between schools and community organisations.

Many schools and community organisations are registered charities, which means that they are eligible to receive charitable donations and may be tax-exempt. Charitable funding can play a significant role in supporting partnerships, but it is important for schools and community organisations to be mindful of the regulations and requirements that come with charitable status.

There are a few key considerations for schools and community organisations when it comes to charitable status and the use of charitable funding for partnerships:

Understanding the regulations: It is important for schools and community organisations to understand the regulations and requirements that come with charitable status, including the rules around fundraising and the use of charitable donations.

Ensuring transparency: Schools and community organisations should be transparent about the use of charitable funding for partnerships, including how the funds are being used and the impact they are having.

Seeking advice: Schools and community organisations should seek advice from legal and financial professionals when necessary to ensure that they are in compliance with the regulations and requirements of charitable status.

By understanding the regulations and requirements of charitable status and being transparent about the use of charitable funding for partnerships, schools and community organisations can ensure that they are able to support partnerships in a way that is effective and compliant with the law.

Implementation in real-world scenarios
Navigating the allocation of charitable funds within partnerships initiatives requires a careful balance between transformative charitable endeavours like bursaries and scholarships, and the support of partnership activities.

While this discussion typically occurs at the board and senior leadership levels, there's no definitive right or wrong answer. Each school, with its unique resources and priorities, may opt to allocate funds differently. The primary consideration lies in ensuring that charitable funds are utilised effectively for charitable purposes.

While education inherently serves a charitable function, it's essential to ensure that funds are directed towards initiatives that benefit the wider community, particularly those in need.

This entails thorough evaluation and monitoring to assess the impact of every pound spent. Regular meetings involving partnerships leads and senior teams across participating schools play a vital role in evaluating the effectiveness of fund allocation. By reviewing the expenditure against the desired outcomes and assessing the achieved impact, schools can ensure that charitable funds are optimally utilised to promote public benefit, social mobility, and the overall success of partnership endeavours.

27: Safeguarding in partnerships

In this section, we will explore the importance of safeguarding in partnerships between schools and community organisations. Safeguarding is the process of protecting children and vulnerable adults from harm, abuse, and neglect, and it is essential for partnerships to ensure that all stakeholders are aware of and adhere to safeguarding practices.

There are a few key considerations for safeguarding in partnerships:

Establishing policies and procedures: Schools and community organisations should establish clear policies and procedures for safeguarding that outline the expectations for all stakeholders. These policies and procedures should be shared with all stakeholders and should be regularly reviewed and updated.

Providing training: Schools and community organisations should provide training on safeguarding to all stakeholders, including students, teachers, and community members. This training should cover topics such as recognising and reporting abuse and neglect, and should be provided on a regular basis.

Monitoring and evaluating: Schools and community organisations should regularly monitor and evaluate the effectiveness of their safeguarding practices to ensure that they are meeting the needs of all stakeholders and are effective at protecting children and vulnerable adults.

By prioritising safeguarding in partnerships, schools and community organisations can ensure that all stakeholders are aware of and adhere to safeguarding practices and that children and vulnerable adults are protected from harm.

Implementation in real-world scenarios
Safeguarding within partnerships demands significant staff investment from both hosting and visiting schools. While approaches vary based on school type, size, and existing policies, adherence to government guidelines is paramount, with all staff sharing responsibility for student safety and well-being.

Regular updates to KCSIE (Keeping Children Safe in Education) are crucial, ensuring staff remain informed and compliant. While the topic is vast, key measures must be addressed to promote awareness and compliance.

Establishing communication between Designated Safeguarding Leads (DSLs) in each school serves as a fundamental starting point. Collaborating on partnership goals and operational procedures allows for the alignment of safeguarding policies and planning for activities involving cross-campus visits.

It is essential to verify the safeguarding training, qualifications, and vetting of accompanying adults. Some partnership groups opt to share certification for seamless staff mobility, while others ensure continuous adult supervision throughout sessions, particularly for sporadic interactions. While it may be tempting to overlook safeguarding for brief activities, partnerships leads must prioritise student safety. Vigilance, respect, and care should underscore all activities, fostering a culture of comprehensive safeguarding awareness and action.

28: Risk assessment in partnerships

In this section, we will explore the importance of risk assessment in partnerships between schools and community organisations.

Risk assessment is the process of identifying and evaluating potential risks to the safety and well-being of all stakeholders, and it is essential for partnerships to ensure that appropriate measures are in place to mitigate these risks.

There are a few key considerations for risk assessment in partnerships:

Identifying potential risks: Schools and community organisations should identify potential risks to the safety and well-being of all stakeholders, including risks related to the activities and programs being implemented, the environment, and the involvement of volunteers.

Evaluating the likelihood and impact of risks: Schools and community organisations should evaluate the likelihood and impact of potential risks to determine the level of risk and the appropriate measures to mitigate it.

Implementing risk mitigation measures: Schools and community organisations should implement appropriate measures to mitigate the risks identified through the risk assessment process. This may involve implementing policies and procedures, providing training, or making changes to the environment or activities.

By conducting risk assessments and implementing appropriate risk mitigation measures, schools and community organisations can ensure that partnerships are safe and supportive environments for all stakeholders.

Implementation in real-world scenarios
It's easy to fall into the trap of recycling old risk assessments, merely updating the date and moving forward. However, partnerships leaders should view risk assessments as valuable processes rather than just paperwork for every activity.

While using a template is acceptable, each event warrants a comprehensive review and discussion to ensure a thorough risk assessment. Schools typically assess likelihood and severity, resulting in a calculated score that highlights areas requiring attention. Based on this evaluation, additional measures may be necessary to mitigate risks, or in some cases, the activity may be deemed too risky to proceed.

Certain scenarios, such as transporting children in a minibus, present potential risks (possible multiple death), but adherence to safety protocols like regular vehicle checks, trained drivers, seatbelt usage, and breakdown procedures significantly reduces these risks.

Prior to each event, a pre-meeting should convene with all supervising adults to discuss the risk assessment, ensuring comprehension and readiness. Throughout and after the activity, the risk assessment should be updated to incorporate any unexpected occurrences, enabling future events to account for these factors.

Sub-procedures, such as accident reporting and allergy checks, are integral components that schools should implement, each tailored to their specific policies and practices.

29: Useful resources for partnerships
In this section, we will explore some useful resources for partnerships between schools and community organisations.

There are many organisations and resources available to support partnerships, including professional organisations, funding sources, and online resources.

Some useful resources for partnerships include:

Professional organisations: There are many professional organisations that provide support and resources for partnerships, such as the Independent Schools Council (ISC), The Schools Partnerships Alliance (SPA) and of course the Schools together website. These organisations often offer training, technical assistance, and networking opportunities for schools and community organisations.

Funding sources: There are a variety of funding sources available to support partnerships, including foundations, government agencies, and corporate sponsors. Schools and community organisations should research the various funding sources available and apply for grants that align with the goals and objectives of their partnerships.

Online resources: There are many online resources available to support partnerships, including websites, blogs, and social media groups. These resources can provide information, inspiration, and support for schools and community organisations looking to build and maintain partnerships. By utilising these and other resources, schools and community organisations can access the support and resources they need to build and maintain strong partnerships.

Implementation in real-world scenarios
Identifying and utilising valuable resources is crucial for the success of partnerships. The specific resources may vary depending on the nature and goals of the collaboration. However, several types of resources commonly enhance partnerships between schools.

Educational materials: Access to textbooks, teaching aids, and digital resources can greatly enrich collaborative learning initiatives. Sharing educational materials ensures equitable access and promotes a comprehensive learning experience.

Skills: Leveraging the expertise of educators and professionals within partner schools can enhance teaching and learning quality. Tapping into subject-specific knowledge, pedagogical expertise, or specialised skills enriches educational experiences.

Facilities and infrastructure: Partner schools may have access to diverse facilities like classrooms, laboratories, sports venues, and performance spaces. Sharing physical spaces expands possibilities for joint projects and extracurricular activities.

Community partnerships: Establishing partnerships with community organisations provides valuable resources and support. Community partners offer access to funding, mentorship, guest speakers, or real-world learning experiences.

Technology and digital tools: Incorporating technology facilitates communication, collaboration, and knowledge-sharing among students and educators. Online platforms enable virtual interactions, project-based learning, and global connections.

Financial support: Securing financial support ensures the sustainability of partnership activities. Funding covers expenses related to transportation, materials, professional development, and program implementation.

Professional development opportunities: Offering professional development enhances educators' capacity to collaborate effectively. Workshops, training sessions, and conferences provide valuable skill-building and networking opportunities.

By leveraging these diverse resources, schools cultivate dynamic partnerships that enrich educational experiences, empower educators, and strengthen community connections.

30: Outreach or partnerships?

The use of the word outreach in the education context has been a topic of debate in recent years. Outreach is often used to describe initiatives or programs that are designed to reach beyond the boundaries of a school or organisation, such as by providing services or resources to the wider community. However, some education professionals argue that the use of the word outreach suggests a one-way relationship in which the school or organisation is providing resources or services to the community, rather than engaging in a true partnership.

One of the main arguments against the use of the word outreach is that it suggests a hierarchical relationship, in which the school or organisation is in a position of power and the community is the recipient of the outreach. This dynamic can be problematic, as it can perpetuate the idea that the community is in need of help or assistance from the school or organisation, rather than being seen as an equal partner.

On the other hand, some education professionals argue that the use of the word outreach is simply a matter of terminology and that it can be used in a way that is respectful and inclusive of the community. They argue that the word outreach can be used to describe initiatives that involve collaboration and mutual benefit, and that it does not necessarily imply a hierarchical relationship.

Ultimately, the decision to use the word outreach or another term such as partnership will depend on the specific context and goals of the initiative or program. It is important for schools and organisations to consider the potential implications of their language and to choose terms that reflect the values and principles of their work.

Implementation in real-world scenarios

In the realm of partnerships, discussions often revolve around resource allocation and the principle of mutuality. It's essential to foster a culture of collaboration rather than perpetuating a divide between schools based on their resources.

While independent schools may typically boast superior facilities such as swimming pools and science labs, this isn't always the case. State schools, regardless of level, can also possess impressive resources, including swimming pools or specialised facilities like science labs.

Moreover, there's often a distinction in staffing, with independent schools frequently having dedicated personnel for partnership initiatives, whereas in state schools, this responsibility may fall on the shoulders of the headteacher or another senior staff member.

The key lies in how outreach is approached and transformed into meaningful partnerships. Instead of simply requesting to use a facility, the emphasis should be on open communication and equitable collaboration. Teachers across partner schools should view each other as peers, with a shared pool of resources available for the benefit of all involved.

It is important to prioritise the needs of students, ensuring fair access to facilities, particularly if they're integral to the host school's curriculum.

By adopting this approach, schools can engage in partnerships without feeling beholden or unequal. It's about recognising the inherent strength in collective resources and leveraging them to enrich the educational experience for all students involved.

Ultimately, partnerships thrive on the exchange of knowledge, resources, and support, with each school contributing in its unique way to the collective benefit.

31: Marketing partnerships

In this section, we will explore the importance of marketing partnerships between schools and community organisations. Marketing partnerships can help to raise awareness about the initiatives and programs being implemented, engage stakeholders, and build support for the partnership.

There are a few key considerations for marketing partnerships:

Identifying the target audience: It is important for schools and community organisations to identify the target audience for their marketing efforts, as this will help to guide the messaging and approach. The target audience may include students, teachers, community members, parents, or other stakeholders.

Developing a marketing plan: Schools and community organisations should develop a marketing plan that outlines the goals and objectives of the marketing efforts, the target audience, the marketing channels that will be used, and the timeline for the campaign.

Implementing marketing activities: Schools and community organisations should implement a range of marketing activities to reach the target audience, such as social media campaigns, email marketing, and public relations efforts. It is important to use a variety of marketing channels to reach as many people as possible.

Evaluating the effectiveness of marketing efforts: Schools and community organisations should regularly evaluate the effectiveness of their marketing efforts to ensure that they are achieving the desired results. This may involve tracking metrics such as website traffic, social media engagement, and event attendance.

By developing and implementing a comprehensive marketing plan, schools and community organisations can build awareness and support for their partnerships and ensure that they have a positive impact on student learning and development.

Implementation in real-world scenarios
Marketing within partnerships is a critical aspect that demands focused attention. Some partnership groups opt to establish a distinct entity, devoid of any single school's branding, to promote a sense of equality among stakeholders.

Conversely, other groups may revolve around a lead school, evident in their logos and marketing materials.

Regardless of the structural setup, as discussed previously, there should be a sense of mutuality across the partnership. Marketing efforts for events and activities should be multifaceted, with each partner employing its own marketing strategies. It's common for schools to cross-promote each other, fostering mutual support and raising awareness of collaborative efforts.

Celebrating achievements and vocalising successes is vital. It not only emphasises the collaborative nature of the partnership but also serves as compelling evidence when seeking sponsorship or funding.

Regular updates for staff, parents, and students keep partnerships at the forefront and serve as excellent conversation starters at various events.

Many partnerships maintain separate social media channels dedicated solely to partnership activities. This approach prevents overwhelming the main school channels while allowing individual schools to showcase their involvement as they see fit. In larger events, effective marketing plays a pivotal role in building a brand and attracting interest from various industries. Post-event, marketing teams can disseminate press releases and manage broadcasting opportunities to further amplify the partnership's impact.

In some cases, secondary schools with dedicated marketing departments may extend support to other schools within the network, offering assistance with messaging and promotional activities. This collaborative approach was particularly evident during the pandemic, where schools could leverage their collective efforts to support one another effectively.

32: Succession planning in partnerships

In this section, we will explore the importance of succession planning in partnerships between schools and community organisations.

Succession planning is the process of identifying and developing the next generation of leaders who will take over the partnership when current leaders retire or move on to other roles.

There are a few key considerations for succession planning in partnerships:

Identifying potential leaders: Schools and community organisations should identify potential leaders within the partnership who have the skills, knowledge, and commitment to take on leadership roles in the future. This may include identifying current staff members or volunteers who show potential or recruiting new leaders from outside the partnership.

Developing leadership skills: Schools and community organisations should provide opportunities for potential leaders to develop the skills and knowledge needed to succeed in leadership roles. This may involve providing training, mentorship, and leadership development programs.

Establishing a succession plan: Schools and community organisations should establish a succession plan that outlines the steps that will be taken to transition leadership to the next generation. This may involve creating job descriptions, setting performance goals, and establishing a timeline for the transition.

By planning for succession, schools and community organisations can ensure that they have a strong leadership pipeline in place to support the ongoing success of the partnership. This can help to ensure that the partnership is able to adapt to changing needs and continue to make a positive impact on student learning and development.

Implementation in real-world scenarios
Succession planning within partnerships is a crucial element that requires careful consideration and proactive management. It involves identifying and developing future leaders within the partnership to ensure continuity and effectiveness.

Rather than simply reacting to changes in personnel, succession planning entails a proactive approach to anticipate and prepare for transitions in leadership roles. This process involves identifying key positions within the partnership and assessing the skills and capabilities required to fill these roles effectively.

Succession planning should be integrated into the overall strategic planning process of the partnership. This means regularly reviewing the current leadership team, identifying potential gaps or areas of concern, and developing strategies to address them.

Effective succession planning involves more than just identifying potential candidates; it also requires investing in their development and providing opportunities for growth and advancement. This may involve mentorship programs, leadership training, and exposure to different aspects of partnership management. Communication is key throughout the succession planning process. It's important to keep all stakeholders informed about upcoming transitions, the rationale behind succession decisions, and the plans in place, to ensure a smooth transition.

Succession planning should be an ongoing process rather than a one-time event. It requires regular review and adjustment to adapt to changing circumstances within the partnership and the broader educational landscape.

33: Approaching local businesses for support

In this section, we will explore the best ways for schools and community organisations to approach local businesses for support in partnerships. Local businesses can be valuable partners for education initiatives, as they can provide resources, expertise, and support to help students learn and grow.

There are a few key considerations for approaching local businesses for support:

Identifying businesses that align with the goals and values of the partnership: Schools and community organisations should identify local businesses that align with the goals and values of the partnership. This may involve researching the mission and values of different businesses and looking for companies that have a track record of supporting education or community initiatives.

Developing a compelling case for support: Schools and community organisations should develop a compelling case for support that explains how the partnership will benefit the business and the community. This may involve outlining the specific needs and goals of the partnership, and explaining how the business can make a difference.

Establishing a clear plan for partnership: Schools and community organisations should establish a clear plan for the partnership that outlines the roles and responsibilities of all stakeholders, as well as the expected outcomes and impact. This will help businesses understand the value of the partnership and what they can expect to gain from their involvement.

By following these steps, schools and community organisations can effectively approach local businesses for support and build strong partnerships that benefit all stakeholders.

Implementation in real-world scenarios
Securing external funding for partnership initiatives is a common challenge faced by schools. While schools often have innovative ideas and some resources, additional financial support is needed to bring these ideas to fruition. However, relying solely on school budgets is often insufficient, necessitating the pursuit of external funding opportunities.

Despite extensive outreach efforts, securing funding from larger companies can be challenging, as many already have established charity partnerships or may not have resources available for small-scale initiatives. Similarly, smaller companies may lack the means to provide financial support. While occasional successes, such as sponsorship for specific events or programs, do occur, they are relatively rare.

Success in securing external funding hinges on building relationships and cultivating trust with potential sponsors. Merely approaching companies for financial support without prior engagement may yield limited results.

Therefore, it's essential to involve local industries in partnership events, advisory groups, and social media promotions to familiarise them with the partnership's objectives and potential impact. Inviting representatives from local businesses to events, treating them as VIPs, and providing opportunities for their staff to engage in partnership activities can foster a sense of connection and investment.

By showcasing the partnership's efforts to address community needs and overcome challenges collaboratively, schools can demonstrate their value to potential sponsors. Maintaining and nurturing these relationships is equally important. Continuously engage with sponsors, provide regular updates on the impact of their contributions, and offer opportunities for them to see firsthand the difference they are making.

Additionally, tailor impact reports and presentations to highlight the specific benefits of their support, further reinforcing their commitment to the partnership.

By actively managing these relationships and demonstrating the tangible outcomes of their support, schools can increase the likelihood of continued sponsorship and foster long-term partnerships with external funders.

34: Explaining the importance of investing in children from other schools

In this section, we will explore how to effectively explain to school staff the importance of investing in children from other schools. Partnering with other schools can provide a range of benefits for students, including increased access to resources, expanded learning opportunities, and the development of skills such as collaboration and communication.

However, some school staff may have concerns or questions about why the school is investing in children from other schools.

There are a few key considerations for explaining the importance of investing in children from other schools to school staff:

Highlighting the benefits for students: It is important to emphasise the benefits that partnering with other schools can provide for students, including increased access to resources, expanded learning opportunities, and the development of skills such as collaboration and communication.

Emphasising the importance of collaboration: Partnering with other schools can help to foster a culture of collaboration and support among schools, which can ultimately benefit all students. It is important to emphasise the importance of working together to improve student learning and development.

Communicating the long-term vision for the partnership: It is important to communicate the long-term vision for the partnership and how it aligns with the school's mission and values. This can help to ensure that school staff understand the bigger picture and how the partnership fits into the overall goals of the school.

By effectively communicating the benefits and importance of partnering with other schools, schools can ensure that school staff understand and support the investment in children from other schools.

Implementation in real-world scenarios
Addressing concerns from parents in the independent school sector regarding the allocation of resources towards partnership activities is a common and valid issue.

Many parents make sacrifices to afford school fees, and seeing funds seemingly directed towards students from other schools can raise questions and concerns.

However, resolving these concerns often requires open communication and a personalised approach. Engaging in direct conversations with concerned parents, explaining the mutual benefits of partnership activities, and highlighting how all students, including those from the independent school, gain valuable experiences and learning opportunities through collaboration can help alleviate apprehensions.

Additionally, providing insights into the funding sources for partnership initiatives, such as charitable funds derived from VAT exemptions, can offer transparency and clarity. However, it's essential to acknowledge that reliance on such funding mechanisms may not always be feasible due to educational policy dynamics.

Ultimately, emphasising the educational value of partnership activities is crucial. Highlighting how experiential learning, exposure to diverse environments and individuals, and the opportunity to develop future workplace skills enrich the educational journey for all students can help parents understand the broader benefits beyond financial considerations.

By fostering understanding and emphasising the positive impacts of partnerships on student learning and development, schools can address parental concerns and reinforce the value of collaborative initiatives in enhancing education for all children.

35: Replacing core services that should be provided by the state

In this section, we will explore the challenges and considerations for schools and community organisations when replacing core services that should be provided by the state.

In some cases, schools and community organisations may find themselves in the position of having to fill gaps in services that are essential for student learning and development, but which are not being provided by the government.

There are a few key considerations for replacing core services that should be provided by the state:

Identifying the gaps in services: Schools and community organisations should assess the needs of their students and communities and identify any gaps in services that are essential for student learning and development. This may involve conducting needs assessments, gathering data, and engaging with stakeholders to understand the specific needs and challenges facing the community.

Developing a plan to address the gaps: Schools and community organisations should develop a plan to address the identified gaps in services. This may involve partnering with other organisations, seeking funding or resources, or implementing new programs or initiatives. It is important to involve all stakeholders in the planning process to ensure that the plan is comprehensive and meets the needs of the community.

Evaluating the effectiveness of the plan: Schools and community organisations should regularly evaluate the effectiveness of their efforts to replace core services that should be provided by the state. This may involve tracking metrics such as student attendance, academic performance, and engagement with the community.

By following these steps, schools and community organisations can effectively address gaps in essential services and support student learning and development. However, it is important to recognise that replacing core services that should be provided by the state is not a sustainable long-term solution, and it is important to advocate for the provision of these services by the government.

Implementation in real-world scenarios
Replacing core services that should be provided by the state with those offered through school partnerships requires careful consideration and caution. While partnerships can play a valuable role in enhancing educational experiences and addressing gaps in

services, they should not serve as a substitute for essential services that are the responsibility of the government.

One of the primary concerns with replacing core services through partnerships is the risk of exacerbating existing inequalities. If certain schools or communities rely heavily on partnerships to access essential services, it can widen disparities between schools with robust partnership networks and those without.

This can perpetuate inequities in education and contribute to a two-tiered system where students in partnership-rich schools receive better resources and support than those in schools without access to such services. Furthermore, relying on partnerships to deliver core services may lead to inconsistencies and gaps in service provision.

Partnerships are often dependent on external funding, volunteer support, or the availability of partner organisations, which can be unpredictable and subject to change. This instability can result in disruptions to essential services and leave students vulnerable to gaps in support.

Another consideration is the potential for partnerships to detract from the primary mission of schools. While partnerships can enrich the educational experience and provide valuable opportunities for students, they should not overshadow the fundamental role of schools in delivering high-quality education. Schools must prioritise their core functions, such as curriculum delivery, student support, and staff development, to ensure that all students receive a comprehensive and equitable education.

Moreover, relying too heavily on partnerships to deliver core services may shift the burden of responsibility away from the government and undermine efforts to advocate for adequate funding and support for public education.

By filling gaps in services through partnerships, there is a risk of normalising underfunding and neglect of public education, rather than addressing systemic issues and advocating for sustainable solutions.

36: Top 10 questions asked by partnerships staff

In this section, we will explore the top 10 questions that are frequently asked by partnerships staff.

Partnerships staff play a critical role in building and maintaining strong collaborations between schools and community organisations, and they often have a range of questions and concerns as they navigate the complexities of partnerships work.

1. How do we identify potential partners?
2. How do we engage stakeholders?
3. How do we manage resources effectively?
4. How do we measure the impact of the partnership?
5. How do we sustain the partnership over time?
6. How do we manage conflicts and challenges?
7. How do we meet the needs of all stakeholders?
8. How do we communicate with stakeholders?
9. How do we build trust and relationships
10. How do we adapt to changing needs/priorities?

By addressing these key questions, partnerships staff can build strong and effective collaborations that support student learning and development.

How do we identify potential partners?
There are a few key steps that schools and community organisations can take to identify potential partners:

Assess the needs of the school or organisation: It is important to assess the needs of the school or organisation and identify areas where partnerships could make a positive impact.

Research potential partners: Schools and community organisations can research potential partners by looking for organisations that align with their values and goals, and that have a track record of success in similar initiatives.

Engage with the community: Schools and community organisations can engage with the community to gather input and ideas about potential partners. This may involve conducting surveys, focus groups, or community meetings.

How do we engage stakeholders in the partnership process?
There are a few key strategies for engaging stakeholders in the partnership process:

Communicate clearly and regularly: It is important to communicate clearly and regularly with stakeholders about the goals and progress of the partnership. This may involve providing updates through newsletters, emails, or social media.

Involve stakeholders in decision-making: Schools and community organisations can involve stakeholders in decision-making by providing opportunities for input and feedback. This may involve holding focus groups, conducting surveys, or establishing advisory committees.

Recognise and value the contributions of stakeholders: Schools and community organisations should recognise and value the contributions of stakeholders by thanking them for their time and effort, and by highlighting their impact on the partnership.

How do we manage resources and budget effectively?
There are a few key strategies for managing resources and budget effectively in partnerships:

Establish clear roles and responsibilities: It is important to establish clear roles and responsibilities for all stakeholders in the partnership, including who is responsible for managing resources and budget.

Develop a budget plan: Schools and community organisations should develop a budget plan that outlines the expected costs and revenues for the partnership. This may involve working with partners to identify funding sources and allocate resources.

How do we measure the impact of the partnership?
Measuring the impact of a partnership can help schools and community organisations understand the effectiveness of their efforts and make improvements as needed.

There are a few key strategies for measuring the impact of a partnership:

Set clear goals and objectives: It is important to set clear goals and objectives for the partnership, as this will help to define what success looks like and provide a basis for measuring impact.

Collect data: Schools and community organisations should collect data on a regular basis to track progress and measure impact. This may involve tracking metrics such as student attendance, academic performance, and engagement with the community.

Engage with stakeholders: Schools and community organisations should engage with stakeholders, including students, teachers, and community members, to gather feedback and insights on the impact of the partnership.

How do we sustain the partnership over time?
Sustaining a partnership over time can be challenging, but there are a few key strategies that schools and community organisations can use to ensure long-term success:

Communicate regularly: It is important to communicate regularly with partners to ensure that everyone is aligned and working towards the same goals. This may involve holding regular meetings, sending updates, or using other forms of communication.

Review and adapt the partnership: Schools and community organisations should regularly review the partnership to assess its effectiveness and identify areas for improvement. This may involve gathering data, engaging with stakeholders, and adapting the partnership as needed.

Foster positive relationships: Building and maintaining positive relationships with partners is key to sustaining a partnership over time. Schools and community organisations should work to foster trust and build strong, collaborative relationships.

How do we manage conflicts and challenges that arise in the partnership?

Conflicts and challenges are a natural part of partnerships work, and it is important for schools and community organisations to have strategies in place to address them. There are a few key strategies for managing conflicts and challenges in partnerships:

Communicate openly and honestly: It is important to communicate openly and honestly with partners about conflicts or challenges that arise. This may involve holding regular meetings to discuss issues and work towards solutions.

Establish clear guidelines for conflict resolution: Schools and community organisations should establish clear guidelines for conflict resolution that outline the steps that will be taken to address conflicts or challenges. This may involve setting up a mediation process or establishing a system for escalating issues as needed.

Foster a culture of collaboration and mutual respect: Building a culture of collaboration and mutual respect among partners can help to prevent conflicts from arising in the first place. Schools and community organisations should work to foster positive relationships and encourage open and respectful communication.

How do we ensure that the partnership is meeting the needs of all stakeholders?

Ensuring that the partnership is meeting the needs of all stakeholders is essential for its success. There are a few key strategies for achieving this:

Engage with stakeholders regularly: Schools and community organisations should engage with stakeholders, including students, teachers, and community members, on a regular basis to gather feedback and insights on the partnership. This may involve holding focus groups, conducting surveys, or hosting community meetings.

Be transparent and open to feedback: Schools and community organisations should be transparent about the goals and progress of the partnership and be open to feedback from stakeholders. This may involve providing regular updates, being responsive to questions and concerns, and welcoming suggestions for improvement.

Adapt to changing needs and priorities: The needs and priorities of stakeholders can change over time, and it is important for schools and community organisations to be flexible and adapt to these changes. This may involve reviewing and updating the partnership regularly to ensure that it is meeting the needs of all stakeholders.

How do we communicate with different stakeholders, including students, parents, teachers, and community members?

Effective communication is key to the success of partnerships, and it is important for schools and community organisations to have strategies in place for communicating with different stakeholders. There are a few key considerations for communicating with different stakeholders:

Identify the needs and preferences of each stakeholder group: Schools and community organisations should identify the needs and preferences of each stakeholder group when it comes to communication. This may involve conducting surveys, holding focus groups, or engaging with stakeholders directly to understand their preferences.

Use a variety of communication channels: Schools and community organizations should use a variety of communication channels to reach different stakeholders, including email, newsletters, social media, and in-person events.

Be transparent and timely: It is important for schools and community organisations to be transparent and timely in their communication with stakeholders. This may involve providing regular updates on the progress of the partnership, being responsive to questions and concerns, and being open to feedback.

How do we build trust and foster positive relationships within the partnership?

Building trust and fostering positive relationships within the partnership is essential for its success. There are a few key strategies for achieving this:

Communicate openly and honestly: It is important to communicate openly and honestly with partners to build trust and foster positive relationships. This may involve holding regular meetings to discuss issues and work towards solutions.

Establish clear guidelines and expectations: Schools and community organisations should establish clear guidelines and expectations for the partnership, including roles and responsibilities, goals and objectives, and protocols for communication and decision-making.

Recognise and value the contributions of partners: Schools and community organisations should recognise and value the contributions of partners by thanking them for their time and effort, and by highlighting their impact on the partnership.

How do we adapt to changing needs and priorities in the partnership?

It is important for schools and community organisations to be flexible and adapt to changing needs and priorities in the partnership. There are a few key strategies for achieving this:

Review and assess the partnership regularly: Schools and community organisations should regularly review and assess the partnership to identify areas for improvement and ensure that it is meeting the needs of all stakeholders. This may involve gathering data, engaging with stakeholders, and adapting the partnership as needed.

Be open to feedback: Schools and community organisations should be open to feedback from stakeholders and be willing to make changes based on that feedback. This may involve conducting surveys, holding focus groups, or hosting community meetings.

Foster a culture of continuous improvement: Schools and community organisations should foster a culture of continuous improvement, which involves regularly seeking out new opportunities for growth and development and being open to change.

37: Fundraising for Partnerships in Education

Partnerships in education can be a powerful tool for improving student outcomes, but they often require financial support in order to be successful.

Fundraising can be a challenging task, but with careful planning and the right strategies, it is possible to secure the resources needed to sustain and grow your partnership.

One effective way to fundraise for partnerships in education is through grant writing. Many foundations and government agencies provide funding for educational programs, and writing a grant proposal is a way to request financial support for your partnership. Grant proposals should clearly outline the goals and objectives of your partnership, as well as the specific activities and initiatives that you will undertake to achieve those goals. It is also important to demonstrate the potential impact of your partnership on student learning and success.

Another way to fundraise for partnerships in education is through partnerships with businesses and corporations. Many companies are willing to support educational initiatives that align with their values and mission and can provide financial support through sponsorships or other forms of support.

It is important to research potential corporate partners and tailor your pitch to their specific interests and priorities.

Community fundraising is another option for supporting partnerships in education. This can involve hosting events, such as bake sales or car washes, or seeking donations from individuals in the community. It can also involve working with local organisations, such as service clubs or faith groups, to secure support for your partnership.

No matter which fundraising strategies you choose, it is important to be strategic and intentional in your efforts. This may involve creating a fundraising plan, setting specific goals and targets, and keeping track of your progress.

By building strong partnerships and engaging in effective fundraising, you can help ensure the long-term success of your educational initiatives and make a lasting impact on student learning and achievement.

38: Matching partnership activity to the curriculum

Partnerships in education can provide a range of benefits for students, including access to resources and experiences that may not be available within the school setting. However, it is important to ensure that partnership activities are aligned with the curriculum and support student learning.

One way to do this is to identify the learning goals and objectives of your partnership and align them with the standards and outcomes outlined in your regions curriculum. This can help ensure that partnership activities are not only enjoyable and engaging for students, but also meaningful and relevant to their academic progress.

It is also important to involve teachers in the planning and implementation of partnership activities. Teachers can provide valuable insight into the needs and interests of their students, as well as the ways in which partnership activities can be integrated into the classroom. By working closely with teachers, you can help ensure that partnership activities support student learning and are effectively integrated into the curriculum.

Finally, it is important to assess the impact of partnership activities on student learning. This can involve gathering feedback from students, teachers, and other stakeholders, as well as collecting data on student performance before and after partnership activities.

By evaluating the effectiveness of your partnership, you can adjust as needed and ensure that your activities are supporting student success.

In summary, matching partnership activity to the curriculum is crucial for ensuring that students can make meaningful connections between their learning and the world around them. By aligning activities with learning goals and involving teachers in the planning process, you can help ensure that your partnership is making a positive impact on student learning and achievement.

39: Targeting real disadvantage and underprivilege in partnerships

Partnerships in education can be a powerful tool for addressing issues of disadvantage and underprivilege, but it is important to approach this work with care and sensitivity.

Here are a few strategies for targeting real disadvantage and underprivilege in your partnerships:

Identify the specific needs of your community: It is important to understand the unique challenges and needs of the community you serve. This may involve gathering data on factors such as poverty rates, access to resources, and academic achievement. By understanding the specific needs of your community, you can tailor your partnership activities to address these issues in a targeted and effective way.

Engage with community members and stakeholders: Building partnerships with community members and stakeholders is essential for addressing issues of disadvantage and underprivilege. This may involve working with community organisations, local businesses, or individuals with lived experience of these issues. Engaging with these groups can help ensure that your partnership activities are informed by the perspectives and needs of the community.

Collaborate with schools and other educational organisations: Partnering with schools and other educational organisations can help you reach a larger number of students and have a greater impact. By collaborating with these groups, you can pool resources and expertise to address issues of disadvantage and underprivilege in a more comprehensive and effective way.

Evaluate and adjust your approach as needed: It is important to regularly assess the impact of your partnership activities on student learning and success. By evaluating your approach, you can identify areas for improvement and adjust as needed to better target real disadvantage and underprivilege.

Targeting real disadvantage and underprivilege in partnerships requires a careful and thoughtful approach. By working with community members and stakeholders, collaborating with schools and other educational organisations, and regularly evaluating your approach, you can make a positive impact on the lives of disadvantaged and underprivileged students.

40: Partnerships and diversity
Partnerships in education can be an effective way to promote diversity and inclusivity within the school setting. By partnering with organisations and individuals from a range of backgrounds and experiences, schools can expose students to diverse perspectives and help create a more inclusive and welcoming environment.

There are a few key strategies for promoting diversity and inclusivity through partnerships:

Seek out diverse partners: Partnering with organisations and individuals that represent a range of backgrounds, experiences, and perspectives can help expose students to diverse viewpoints and experiences. This may involve partnering with community groups, cultural organisations, or businesses that are owned and operated by individuals from underrepresented groups.

Foster open communication and dialogue: Building trust and understanding between diverse partners requires open and honest communication. Encourage open dialogue and encourage all partners to share their perspectives and experiences. This can help create a more inclusive and welcoming environment for all.

Encourage student involvement: Involving students in the planning and implementation of partnership activities can help them feel more invested in the process and encourage a sense of ownership and belonging. Encourage students to bring their own experiences and perspectives to the table and involve them in decision-making processes.

Reflect on and assess your approach: It is important to regularly assess the impact of your partnership activities on diversity and inclusivity. This may involve gathering feedback from students, teachers, and community members, as well as collecting data on student diversity and engagement. By reflecting on your approach, you can identify areas for improvement and adjust as needed.

Partnerships can be an effective way to promote diversity and inclusivity within the school setting. By seeking out diverse partners, fostering open communication and dialogue, and involving students in the process, you can help create a more inclusive and welcoming environment for all.

41: The best characteristics and skills of partnerships staff

Partnerships in education require a range of skills and characteristics in order to be successful. Here are a few key qualities that can help partnerships staff be effective in their roles:

Strong communication skills: Partnerships staff should be able to clearly and effectively communicate with a variety of stakeholders, including teachers, students, community members, and other partners. This may involve communicating through a range of mediums, such as email, phone, or in-person meetings.

Adaptability and flexibility: Partnerships can involve a range of activities and initiatives, and partnerships staff should be able to adapt to changing needs and demands. This may involve being open to new ideas, being willing to try new approaches, and being able to pivot quickly when necessary.

Strong organisational skills: Partnerships staff should be able to manage multiple tasks and responsibilities at once, and should be able to prioritise tasks and stay organised. This may involve creating and maintaining schedules, tracking progress, and keeping track of resources.

Relationship-building skills: Partnerships involve working with a variety of individuals and organisations, and partnerships staff should be able to build strong relationships with these partners. This may involve networking, building trust, and being able to effectively collaborate with others.

Cultural competency: Partnerships often involve working with individuals and organisations from a range of backgrounds, and partnerships staff should be able to work effectively with people from diverse cultures and experiences. This may involve understanding and respecting different cultural practices and norms and being able to communicate effectively across cultural divides.

Partnerships staff should possess a range of skills and characteristics in order to be effective in their roles. By having strong communication skills, being adaptable and flexible, being well-organised, having strong relationship-building skills, and being culturally competent, partnerships staff can help ensure the success of their partnerships and make a positive impact on student learning and achievement.

42: Avoiding the "Robin Hood" approach in partnerships

The "Robin Hood" approach in partnerships refers to the practice of taking resources from one group or area and redistributing them to another, without addressing the root causes of inequality or disadvantage.

While it is important to address issues of inequality and disadvantage, the "Robin Hood" approach can be problematic because it does not address the underlying issues and can create dependency.

Here are a few strategies for avoiding the "Robin Hood" approach in partnerships:

Focus on root causes: Instead of simply redistributing resources, work to understand and address the root causes of inequality and disadvantage. This may involve addressing systemic issues such as lack of access to education or healthcare or working to empower marginalised communities through capacity building and leadership development.

Involve community members and stakeholders: Engage with community members and stakeholders in the planning and implementation of partnership activities. This can help ensure that the needs and priorities of the community are being met and can help build local ownership and sustainability.

Encourage self-sufficiency: While it is important to provide support and resources to disadvantaged communities, it is also important to encourage self-sufficiency and independence. This may involve providing skills training and other forms of support to help individuals and communities become more self-sufficient and self-reliant.

Evaluate and adjust your approach: Regularly assess the impact of your partnership activities on inequality and disadvantage, and make adjustments as needed. This may involve gathering feedback from community members and stakeholders, as well as collecting data on outcomes and progress.

It is important to avoid the "Robin Hood" approach in partnerships and instead focus on addressing the root causes of inequality and disadvantage. By involving community members, encouraging self-sufficiency, and regularly evaluating your approach, you can help create lasting and sustainable change.

43: Bringing the school board on the partnerships journey

Partnerships in education can be a powerful tool for improving student outcomes, but it is important to involve the school board in the planning and implementation process.

Here are a few strategies for bringing the school board on the partnerships journey:

Communicate the benefits of partnerships: It is important to clearly communicate the benefits of partnerships to the school board. This may include information on how partnerships can improve student learning and achievement, as well as the potential cost savings and other benefits that partnerships can provide.

Engage the school board in the planning process: Involving the school board in the planning process can help ensure that partnerships align with the regions, goals and objectives. This may involve presenting information on potential partners, outlining the specific activities and initiatives that will be undertaken, and seeking feedback and input from school board members.

Involve the school board in the evaluation process: Regularly updating the school board on the progress and impact of partnerships can help demonstrate their value and build support for future partnerships. This may involve presenting data on student outcomes, gathering feedback from teachers and other stakeholders, and highlighting any cost savings or other benefits that partnerships have provided.

Build relationships with school board members: Building relationships with school board members can help build support for partnerships. This may involve meeting with individual board members, inviting them to participate in partnership activities, and keeping them informed of progress and developments.

In conclusion, involving the school board in the partnerships journey is crucial for ensuring that partnerships align with the region's goals and objectives, and for building support for future partnerships.

By communicating the benefits of partnerships, engaging the school board in the planning process, involving them in the evaluation process, and building relationships with board members, you can help ensure the success of your partnerships and make a positive impact on student learning and achievement.

44: Convincing finance to support partnerships
Securing financial support for partnerships can be a challenge, but it is an essential step in ensuring the success of your initiatives.

Here are a few strategies for convincing finance to support partnerships:

Clearly articulate the benefits of partnerships: It is important to clearly communicate the benefits of partnerships to finance professionals. This may include information on how partnerships can improve student learning and achievement, as well as any cost savings or other financial benefits that partnerships may provide.

Provide data and evidence of the impact of partnerships: Finance professionals are often more likely to support initiatives that have a proven track record of success. By gathering data on the impact of your partnerships, you can demonstrate their value and make a stronger case for financial support.

Identify potential funding sources: Research potential funding sources, such as grants, sponsorships, or other forms of financial support, and present these options to finance professionals. This can help show that there are viable options for funding partnerships and that the investment is likely to pay off in the long run.

Involve finance professionals in the planning process: Involving finance professionals in the planning process can help ensure that partnerships align with the organisation's financial goals and objectives. This may involve seeking input and feedback on budgeting and funding strategies, and working together to develop a plan that meets the needs of both parties.

Convincing finance to support partnerships requires clear communication, data and evidence of impact, and a willingness to involve finance professionals in the planning process. By taking these steps, you can build a strong case for financial support and help ensure the success of your partnerships.

45: How can school staff get involved in partnerships?
There are a number of ways in which school staff can get involved in partnerships:

Identify potential partners: School staff can play a key role in identifying potential partners and building relationships with those organisations. This may involve research, networking, and outreach to organisations that align with the school's goals and objectives.

Involve teachers in the planning process: Teachers can provide valuable insight into the needs and interests of their students, as well as the ways in which partnership activities can be integrated into the curriculum. Involving teachers in the planning process can help ensure that partnerships are meaningful and relevant to student learning.

Support student involvement: Encourage students to get involved in partnership activities and support their participation. This may involve helping students develop leadership skills, facilitating opportunities for students to engage with partners, and providing support and resources as needed.

Facilitate communication and collaboration:
Partnerships often involve working with a range of individuals and organisations, and school staff can help facilitate communication and collaboration between these groups.

This may involve coordinating meetings and other communication channels and working to build strong relationships between partners.

Participate in the evaluation process: School staff can play a key role in assessing the impact of partnerships on student learning and success. This may involve gathering feedback from students, teachers, and other stakeholders, as well as collecting data on student performance before and after partnership activities.

School staff can play a key role in partnerships by identifying potential partners, involving teachers in the planning process, supporting student involvement, facilitating communication and collaboration, and participating in the evaluation process. By taking an active role in partnerships, school staff can help ensure their success and make a positive impact on student learning and achievement.

46: Involving teachers, support staff, and students in partnerships

Partnerships in education can be a powerful tool for improving student outcomes, and involving teachers, support staff, and students in the process can help ensure their success.

Here are a few strategies for getting these groups involved in partnerships:

Involve teachers in the planning process: Teachers can provide valuable insight into the needs and interests of their students, as well as the ways in which partnership activities can be integrated into the curriculum. Involving teachers in the planning process can help ensure that partnerships are meaningful and relevant to student learning.

Engage support staff in partnership activities: Support staff, such as guidance counsellors, school nurses, and librarians, can play a key role in supporting partnership activities and helping to ensure their success. This may involve providing resources, coordinating logistics, or helping to facilitate communication between partners.

Encourage student involvement: Partnerships can provide students with valuable learning experiences and opportunities to develop leadership skills. Encourage students to get involved in partnership activities and support their participation. This may involve helping students develop skills such as communication, collaboration, and problem-solving.

Foster open communication and dialogue: Encourage open communication and dialogue between teachers, support staff, students, and partners. This can help build trust and understanding and can help ensure that partnership activities are meaningful and relevant to all stakeholders.

Evaluate and adjust your approach: Regularly assess the impact of your partnership activities on student learning and success. This may involve gathering feedback from students, teachers, and support staff, as well as collecting data on student performance before and after partnership activities.

By evaluating your approach, you can adjust as needed to better meet the needs of all stakeholders.

47: What is an MOU?

A 'Memorandum of Understanding' (MOU) is a document that outlines the terms and general understanding of a partnership between two or more parties. It is a non-binding agreement that sets out the objectives and responsibilities of each party involved in the partnership, as well as any expectations for the partnership's success.

An MOU is typically used in partnerships that involve a joint venture, collaboration, or cooperation between organisations or individuals. The MOU is not a legally binding document, but it does serve as a formal record of the partnership's goals and objectives, as well as the commitments of each party involved.

An MOU typically includes the following information:

- The names and contact information of the parties involved.
- A description of the partnership's objectives and goals
- The roles and responsibilities of each party
- The expectations for the partnership's success
- The duration of the partnership
- A statement indicating that the MOU is not legally binding.

It is important to note that an MOU should be signed by authorised representatives of each party involved in the partnership.

This serves as evidence of the partnership and the commitment of each party to the partnership's objectives. An MOU can be a useful tool for organisations looking to enter a partnership. It provides a clear understanding of the partnership's goals and objectives, as well as the commitments of each party involved.

This can help to ensure that all parties are on the same page and working towards the same goals, which can increase the chances of the partnership's success.

A Memorandum of Understanding (MOU) is a document used to establish the general understanding of a partnership, outlining the objectives and responsibilities of each party and the expectations of success. It is a non-binding agreement but serves as a formal record of the partnership.

48: What is a 'Partnerships Agreement'?

A 'Partnership Agreement' is a legally binding contract that defines the terms and conditions of a partnership between two or more individuals or organisations. It outlines the rights, responsibilities, and obligations of each party involved in the partnership, as well as the management and operation of the partnership.

A Partnership Agreement typically includes the following information:

- The names and contact information of the partners
- The purpose and scope of the partnership
- The contributions of each partner, including any capital contributions or property
- The distribution of profits and losses among the partners

- The management and decision-making process of the partnership
- The procedures for admitting new partners or dissolving the partnership.
- Provisions for resolving disputes among the partners.

It is important to note that a Partnership Agreement should be tailored to the specific needs and goals of the partnership. It should be clear, concise, and easy to understand for all parties involved.

One of the key benefits of a Partnership Agreement is that it establishes a clear understanding of the partnership's goals and objectives, as well as the commitments of each party involved. This can help to ensure that all partners are on the same page and working towards the same goals, which can increase the chances of the partnership's success.

A Partnership Agreement also serves as a protection for the partners. It establishes rules and procedures for resolving disputes, managing the partnership and dissolving the partnership. This can help to minimise potential conflicts and legal issues that may arise within the partnership. Partnership Agreement is a legally binding contract that outlines the terms and conditions of a partnership.

It defines the rights, responsibilities, and obligations of each party involved, as well as the management and operation of the partnership. It should be tailored to the specific needs and goals of the partnership and serves as protection for the partners and a clear understanding of the partnership's objectives.

49: Resilience as a partnerships member of staff

Resilience is the ability to adapt and bounce back from adversity, and it is an essential skill in partnerships between schools.

Partnerships between schools can be complex and dynamic, and they often involve multiple stakeholders with different goals and perspectives. In such an environment, it is crucial for individuals and organisations to be resilient to navigate the challenges and obstacles that may arise.

One of the main reasons why resilience is needed in partnerships between schools is that partnerships often involve working with people from different backgrounds, cultures and perspectives. Resilience allows individuals and organisations to adapt to these differences and to find common ground to work on. This can help to ensure that partnerships are successful and that the needs of all stakeholders are met.

Another reason why resilience is needed in partnerships between schools is that partnerships can be subject to unexpected changes or setbacks. Resilience allows individuals and organisations to adapt to these changes and to find new solutions. This is important in order to ensure that partnerships are able to continue to meet the needs of students and other stakeholders.

Resilience also plays a critical role in addressing conflicts and misunderstandings that may arise within a partnership. When conflicts or misunderstandings occur, it can be easy to become discouraged or to give up on the partnership. However, resilient individuals and organisations can work through these challenges and find solutions that benefit all parties involved.

Another important aspect of resilience in partnerships between schools is the ability to learn from failures and challenges. Resilient individuals and organisations can learn from their mistakes and use that knowledge to improve their partnerships in the future. This is a crucial aspect of partnerships, as it allows organisations to continuously improve and adapt to changing needs. Resilience is a much-needed skill in partnerships between schools.

50: How to overcome transport issues with partnerships work.

Transportation can be a significant obstacle for partnerships between schools, as it can be difficult and expensive to arrange transportation for students and staff to travel to partner schools.

However, there are several strategies that can be used to overcome transportation issues and ensure that partnerships are successful.

One of the most effective ways to overcome transportation issues is to utilise technology. Virtual partnerships, such as video conferencing and online collaboration tools, can be used to connect students and staff from different locations without the need for physical transportation. This can help to save time and money and reduce the environmental impact of transportation.

Another strategy for overcoming transportation issues is to plan and schedule transportation well in advance.

This can help to ensure that transportation is available when it is needed and that costs are minimised.

Consider different options for transportation such as carpooling, biking, public transportation and more. It is also important to seek out funding or grants for transportation. Many organisations and government agencies provide funding for transportation for educational purposes. Schools can also partner with local businesses, such as transportation companies, to help cover the costs of transportation.

Another strategy is to develop partnerships with other schools in the same area. This can help to reduce transportation costs by allowing students and staff to travel shorter distances to visit partner schools. Finally, it is important to involve students, staff and parents in the process of overcoming transportation issues. They can provide valuable insights and suggestions for how to manage transportation and can also help to generate support for the partnership.

Conclusion

As we conclude this reference book, it is crucial to underscore the immense value inherent in forging connections between schools. These relationships often blossom into organic partnership activities, driven by our collective commitment to nurturing the well-being and growth of the children under our care.

Should your organisation choose to expand its collaborative efforts, strategic planning becomes paramount. Embracing the theory of change and delineating clear outcomes as metrics for success lay the foundation for effective scaling. Thoughtfully designing the structure of your partnerships program early on is essential to circumvent potential challenges down the road, ensuring smooth progress and impactful outcomes.

While partnerships may begin modestly, with limited resources and staff time, it's imperative to recognise that scaling activity necessitates substantial investment in both funding and personnel. However, amidst these considerations, it is crucial to acknowledge the wealth of support and expertise generously offered by peers and colleagues, both locally and globally.

In closing, let us remain steadfast in our commitment to collaboration, innovation, and the holistic development of our educational ecosystems.

Together, we can continue to shape a future where every child has the opportunity to thrive and succeed, empowered by the strength of our partnerships and collective efforts.

Printed in Great Britain
by Amazon